PENGUIN BOOKS

LIFEMANSHIP

Stephen Potter was born in 1900 and educated at Westminster School and Merton College, Oxford, where he read English. In 1926 he became a lecturer in English at London University, and in 1938 he joined the staff of the B.B.C. as a writer-producer. There he became editor of literary features and poetry, and in 1943 Chairman of the Literary Committee. His principal programmes were the 'How' series (with Joyce Grenfell) and Professional Portraits, and he was originator and editor of the New Judgement series. He was also dramatic critic of the *New Statesman*, book critic of the *News Chronicle* and editor of the *Leader Magazine*. His books include *D. H. Lawrence* (1930), *The Nonesuch Coleridge* (1934), *Minnow among Tritons: Letters of Mrs S. T. Coleridge* (1934), *Coleridge and S.T.C.* (1935), *The Muse in Chains: A Study in Education* (1937), *The Theory and Practice of Gamesmanship* (1947), *Lifemanship* (1950), *One-Upmanship* (1952), *Sense of Humour* (anthology; 1954), *Potter on America* (1956), *Supermanship* (1958), *Steps to Immaturity* (1959), *Anti-Woo* (1965), *The Complete Golf Gamesmanship* (1968) and *Pedigree: The Evolution of English Native Words* (1968). Stephen Potter died in 1969.

SAGERDOS DUX VATES
PARENS ET GONJUX.

OUR FOUNDER
(In the background, Station Road, Yeovil)

SOME NOTES ON

LIFEMANSHIP

WITH A SUMMARY OF RECENT RESEARCHES IN

GAMESMANSHIP

BY

STEPHEN POTTER

*

Reprinted from *The Lifemanship Papers*: / 28 Studies
in advanced Lifemanship. / The Bude Lectures. /
Printed for the Lifemanship Association by the
Bude Lectures on Lifemanship Trust. / 681 Station
Road, Yeovil.

*

ILLUSTRATED BY LT.-COL.
FRANK WILSON

PENGUIN BOOKS

Penguin Books Ltd, Harmondsworth, Middlesex, England
Penguin Books, 625 Madison Avenue, New York, New York 10022, U.S.A.
Penguin Books Australia Ltd, Ringwood, Victoria, Australia
Penguin Books Canada Ltd, 2801 John Street, Markham, Ontario, Canada L3R 1B4
Penguin Books (N.Z.) Ltd, 182–190 Wairau Road, Auckland 10, New Zealand

—

First published by Rupert Hart-Davis 1950
Published in Penguin Books 1962
Reprinted 1962, 1964, 1977

—

—

Made and printed in Great Britain by
Hazell Watson & Viney Ltd, Aylesbury, Bucks
Set in Linotype Georgian

To Anon

CONTENTS

7

CONTENTS

ACKNOWLEDGEMENT

Certain chapters of this book originally appeared in *Punch*, and are reproduced here by kind permission of the proprietors. Certain others appeared in the *Sunday Times*, *Lilliput*, the *Journal of the Playing Fields Association*, and the *Atlantic Monthly*. To the proprietors and editors of these also we give thanks.

AUTHOR'S NOTE

I have reprinted these lectures more or less as they were delivered. I have not thought it worth while making the small alterations deemed necessary. Any inaccuracies or repetitions must be put down to the exigencies of the platform — to the essential difference between the Written Word, which is inscribed, and the Spoken Word, which is, essentially, speech

INTRODUCTION

MILLIONS of people have formulated the wish, often unexpressed, that the lessons learnt from the philosophy of Gamesmanship should be extended to include the simple problems of everyday life.

It has been, indeed, a wonderful surprise to me to find that my little book has sown the seed in so many and, if possible, in such tremendously diverse hearts: that it has been popular both with the extremely young and the extremely old – perhaps more so. And maybe it is true that today we stand in need of precisely that kind of formulation, more actual if only because it is less concrete, which finds its expression in the contrastingly manifested *temporal* problems, themselves reflections of a wider principle, which is yet capable of a not less personal approach.

WHAT DOES LIFEMANSHIP MEAN?

Easy question to pose, difficult to answer in a phrase. A way of life, pervading each thought and conditioning our every action? Yes, but something much more, even though it only exists, as a pervasion, intermittently. 'How to live' – yes, but the phrase is too negative. In one of the unpublished notebooks of Rilke * there is an unpublished phrase which might be our text: '. . . if you're not one up (*Bitzleisch*) you're . . . one down (*Rotzleisch*).'

How to be one up – how to make the other man feel that something has gone wrong, however slightly. The Lifeman is never caddish himself, but how simply and

* See page 73 under 'O.K.-names'.

certainly, often, he can make the other man feel a cad, and over prolonged periods.

The great principle of Gamesmanship we know. More humbly but not less ardently, if still on the lower rungs of the ladder, comes the Lifeman, pursuing each petty ploy till he, too, has achieved this 'state of One Upness', this *Bitzleischstüsse*.

WHO IS THE LIFEMAN?

'You, me, all of us.' That is the answer. But there is another answer, too. It is to be found in the presence and existence of the accredited or practising Lifeman, entitled so to be called. A small band yet a growing one,* we work from half a dozen centres coordinated, of course, from our 'H.Q.' at Station Road, Yeovil. Every post brings its new crop of notes, reports, postcards of all kinds, and *ana* out of which, cut to the bone, this conspectus of work in progress has been made.

Day by day our centres send out young men, yes and women too, to assess the lifemanship approach for each district, relatively to the stratum or mode of life incorporated within that district, and suitable to it.

You will find your Lifeman, I hope, genial, encouraging, and, provided you are ready to accept the One Down condition, sometimes apparently genuinely helpful. Yet they are always alert and ready for the slight put-off, the well-timed provocation, which will get the other fellow down.

* According to Hulton Research, the number of lifemen who drink tea but never buy fireworks is 79 (correct for income-group B up to June 1946). The figure for those who are interested in soap substitutes and have not yet been to Portugal is, however, 385.

INTRODUCTION

OPENING REMARKS OF GATTLING-FENN

It is the ordinary, simple everyday things of life, wherein each one of us can, by ploy or gambit, most naturally gain the advantage. When I speak, for instance, of the Opening Remarks of Gattling-Fenn, I am referring to that great Lifeman Harry Gattling-Fenn, and his opening remarks.

With his ready smile and friendly face, his hair artificially tousled, his informal habit of wearing a well-cut old tie round his waist instead of braces, and his general air of geniality, Gattling seemed permanently in the off-guard position. It was only by his *opening remarks*, his power of creating a sense of dis-ease, that one realized, as one used to say of him, that Gattling was *always in play*.

To a young person, for instance, who came to visit him he would say, genially of course, 'Sit you down.' Why was this putting off? Was it the tone? Then if the young man nervously took out a cigarette he would say, 'Well, if you're smoking, I will.'

He would say, 'You want a wash, I expect,' in a way which suggested that he had spotted two dirty fingernails. To people on the verge of middle age he would say, 'You're looking very fit and young.' To a definitely older man, of his still older wife he would comment that he was glad she 'was still moving very briskly about'.

In conversation he would lead people to tell stories against their friends and then, when his turn came to speak, he would say (speaking as always from the point of view of a good-natured man) that he 'wished B. was here' because he 'never told stories behind people's backs'.

Thus a 'lifeman's wicket' was prepared – i.e. a sense of distrust, uncertainty, and broken flow, and Gattling would be in a position to prepare some more paralysing thrust.

'A LITTLE CLUB AT HAYWARD'S HEATH'

It was four years ago that I first saw Gattling in action. It was at Hayward's Heath, I remember, at a sort of social club we had formed, a get-together of people back from Burma, where I, in fact, had never actually been.

The atmosphere was meant to be one of jolly reminiscence. We were drawn together by a mutual interest in Gamesmanship, and a curiosity about the genuineness of each other's war records. 'Lifemanship', as a word, had not then been invented. The atmosphere was pleasant, easy – apparently invincibly so. How well I shall always remember the quietness, the deftness of touch, with which Gattling dried us all up.

There was one ploy of Gattling's which I found particularly effective, and I believe it must have been about this time that I first murmured to myself the word 'Lifemanship'.*

Some of us, though not in fact me, had had some pretty hair-raising experiences on active service; whereas the most dangerous thing that had happened to Gattling, I knew to my certain knowledge, was firewatching outside Sale, two miles beyond the raiding area of Manchester. Without actually lying, Gattling was able to tell the story of this totally uninteresting event, in the presence of three submariners and a man who had been twice captured by and had twice escaped from the Japanese, and to tell it in such a way that these people began apologizing for their relatively comfortable war. 'My God,' said Commander Wright, 'I never realized it was like that.'

'I stamped out the flaming stuff with my foot,' said

* It was certainly not later than November 1947.

Fig. 1. 'A little club at Hayward's Heath'. The curious may be interested to know that the northern side of the room (right-hand window) was 'committee corner', with table and chairs. The left side, scene of the original 'incident', was kept clear for general talk and friendly argle-bargle.

Gattling. Some cinder from a small and distant incendiary had, by a stroke of luck, landed in his garden. 'It wasn't a question of feeling frightened, I just found myself doing it. It was as if somebody else was acting in my person.'

He had eventually buried the cinder with a small trowel.

'It was as if I was in a dream,' said Gattling.

For all my admiration, I really couldn't let Gattling get away with this. 'While Mostyn, here, was raiding St Nazaire,' I said. . . .

'Oh, my God, don't I know it,' said Gattling. 'Those chaps were risking their lives not only every day, but every hour of the day and night. That's why one longed to be doing, doing, doing something. To make some contribution. And that is why I was glad, that day at Sale. . . .' And so on, for another three or four minutes. I got angrier than ever. But I must say I mentally took off my hat to Gattling, not because he probably did less, during the last war, than anybody I met or could even imagine,* but because the mere fact that I was getting angry made me realize that here, in Gattling, was our little science of Gamesmanship bearing new fruit. A new colony had been added to Gamesmanship's Empire.

* Gattling had more than one way of suggesting that he had been 'rather in the thick of things' during the war. For wear in the Sale Home Guard he managed to fiddle a tropical bush shirt. When he began to wear this over corduroy trousers while playing croquet in peace-time, it was noted that the shoulder straps seemed to be scored with the markings of the removed insignia of a brigadier, and there was an unfaded portion on the left breast which looked like the tracery of four rows of medals.

It was small justification to reply, when challenged, that the device was in direct imitation of a gambit invented by R. Hart-Davis.

I

CONVERSATIONSHIP

And now, in the next three chapters, we get down to Lifemanship Basic. Read through quickly for the general sense, and then back to the beginning to memorize each individual gambit. It is not easy, but you will enjoy the small discipline.

In conversation play, the important thing is to get in early and stay there. There are always some slow or feeble-witted people in any conversation group who will turn their heads towards the *man who gets going first*. Any good average Lifeman should be able to succeed here. A simple method is to ask a question and answer it almost immediately yourself, after one person has said 'Oh' – or 'Well'. E.g.:

LIFEMAN: I wonder what the expectation of life of, say, an advertising agent of thirty really is – at this moment of time, I mean.

Having read up the answer to this question * in *Whitaker's Almanack* just before coming into the room, Lifeman, after only a second's pause, can answer his own question.

Another *opening*, more difficult to guard against, is

* But remember that each gambit has its answer or *counterlife*. Do not be downed by the difficulty of Lifeman's question, but answer back with a will *before* he has had time to answer himself. Thus:

COUNTERLIFE: (i) 'I should have thought that question had lost validity in our contemporary context' *or* (ii) 'I wondered how long it would be before somebody asked that question.'

the encouraging personal remark aimed at your chief rival, e.g. 'Good lord, how do you always manage to look so *well*?' There are many variants. 'I'm glad to see you looking so fit' can suggest that at last your friend has cut down to a bottle of whisky a day. More subtle, and more difficult to answer is:

LIFEMAN: You're looking wonderfully relaxed.

I have noted J. Pinson's reply (known as 'Pinson's Reply') to this clever gambit:

LIFEMAN: You're looking wonderfully relaxed ... I thought something good had happened to you.
PINSON: You're looking tremendously relaxed, too.
LIFEMAN (*counter-riposting*): Ah, but I'm not looking nearly so relaxed as you are.
PINSON: Oh, I don't think I'm very relaxed.
LIFEMAN: Oh, yes you are.

Two lifemen may go on in this way for twenty minutes, but to a layman the statement that he is relaxed can suggest that normally he is nervy and abstracted, if not on the verge of a breakdown.

GLACIATION

This is the name for the set of gambits which are designed to induce an awkward silence, or at any rate a disinclination to talk, on the part of possible opponents. The 'freezing' effects of these gambits is sometimes of immense power, and I list them here in order of strength, placing the weakest first:

(*a*) Tell a funny story (not advised).
(*b*) If someone else tells a funny story, do not, whatever happens, tell your own funny story in reply, but

listen intently and not only refrain from laughing or smiling, but make no response, change of expression or movement whatever. The teller of the funny story, whatever the nature of his joke, will then suddenly feel that what he has said is in bad taste. Press home your advantage. If he is a stranger, and has told a story about a man with one leg, it is no bad thing to pretend that one of

Fig. 2. Suggested simulation of false or badly lamed leg, for the Bad Taste gambit in Counter Funny Story play (see text).

your own legs is false, or at any rate that you have a severe limp. This will certainly silence Opponent for the rest of the evening.

(c) 'Spenserian Stunser' – this is the facetious name for Quotationship. The nickname probably arose because the quotation of two or three lines of a stanza from Spenser's *Faery Queen* is probably as good an all-round silencer as anything.*

* It is best for beginners to stick to Spenser. Students who wish to experiment should beware of pitfalls. In general, the older and

(*d*) Languaging up. To 'language up' an opponent is, according to Symes' *Dictionary of Lifemanship and Gameswords*, 'to confuse, irritate and depress by the use of foreign words, fictitious or otherwise, either singly or in groups.'

The standard and still the best method is the gradual. If the subject is the relative methods of various orchestral conductors, for instance, say something early on about the '*tentade*' of Boult. Three minutes later contrast the '*fuldenbiener*' of Kubelik, and the firm '*austag, austag*' of his beat 'which Brahms would have delighted in'.

A general uneasiness should now be developing and

---

more classic the quotations, the more depressing the effect; but they should not be too well known, or they may be taken for a joke. It's no good just saying 'The play's the thing,' for instance, whenever the conversation changes to the subject of a play. And do not, if somebody mentions Italy and Florence, quote Browning: 'Florence lay out on the mountain side,' for this may merely raise an easy laugh – the last thing you want to do.

No, let your quotation be apt and obviously classic. If someone shows signs of capturing attention and admiration by travelmanship, for instance, he can be undermined thus:

TRAVELLER: I'm just back from Florence, too. Where did you stay?

LAYGIRL: An excellent little hotel, recommended by Cook's. Quite cheap. Near the station. Pensione Inglese. It was quite nice. Do you know it?

TRAVELLER: Well – I never stay *in* Florence . . . too noisy . . . and surprisingly suburban . . . but Cyril Waterford lets me use his rambling old castle just beyond Fiesole. Very haunted, very beautiful, five ancient retainers – and fun.

LIFEMAN: Ah – 'Give me a castle, precipice encurled, in a gap of the wind-grieved Apennines.'

Traveller, who has been scoring all along the line against the Laygirl, made to feel awkward about her wretched English-speaking Pension, finds himself entombed in the wave of silence which follows this.

the Lifeman may well feel he has done enough. But for Advanced Languaging I recommend the Macintosh Finisher, invented by H. Macintosh, the tea planter. During one of the lengthening pauses, he will quote one of seventeen genuine *Ballades* in Medieval French which he has learnt by heart. 'Of course, you know this,' he begins ...

> '*Ah, vieille septance du mélange*'

and so on, with reverberating accents on the silent 'e'. After two of these, half his audience will be completely silent for fifteen minutes and the rest may actually have gone.

There is a rare counter to this which I have heard once brilliantly used with wonderful effect by B. Meynell, son of F. Meynell the Gamesman, when he was a mere lad of eighteen. This is to tell, *as if to brighten the atmosphere*, a funny story *in French*. If I had to choose an example of brilliance in Lifemanship it would, I think, be this. For as a cover to any lack of knowledge of the language or the accent, he told it, or made as if to tell it, 'in a strong dialect'.

'Il a répondu "Favoori", in the Toulouse drawl.'

I have never been able to discover whether this was a genuine Toulouse accent or not, nor, indeed, whether B. Meynell can speak any genuine French at all.

(*e*) If the Lifeman is a late-comer and the conversation is already well established, a different gambit-sequence altogether must, of course, be used. In order to *stop the flow* he must judge the *source of eloquence* and deflect the current into a *new channel* by *damming the stream*.*

If, for instance, someone is being really funny or witty

---

* There is a *physical* method of making the too eloquent and successful speaker self-conscious and causing him, in the end, to break down. In brief the ploy is:

(1) To watch not the man but his gestures – his moving hands.

and there is a really pleasant atmosphere of hearty and explosive laughter, then (a) join in the laughter at first. Next (b) gradually become silent. Finally (c) at some pause in the conversation be overheard whispering, 'Oh for some real talk.'

Alternatively, if there is genuinely good conversation and argument, listen silently with exaggerated solemnity and then whisper to your neighbours, 'I'm sorry but I've got a hopeless and idiotic desire to be a little bit silly.'

I strongly recommend this last phrase which indeed might be dignified as a Gambit, though it is usually regarded as a ploy of Lowbrowmanship, which we may discuss under the even more main heading of Writership and Critic Play.

But never forget the uses of Lowbrowmanship in conversation and the phrases 'Oh, I don't know' and 'I'm awfully sorry.' Thus:

LAYMAN: I don't advise the new musical. It's certainly a leg show, but the harmonies are trite, the dialogue is unfunny, and the *décor* is just a splurge.

LOWBROWMAN: Oh, I don't know, I rather like a good bit of old-fashioned vulgarity. And I'm awfully sorry but I like leg shows.

If the Lowbrowman happens to be a Professor of Aesthetics, as he usually is, his remark is all the more irritating.*

(2) To alter the position of some flower-pot, suggesting by your way of doing it (a) That some movement of his hand may be going to knock it over; (b) That these gestures are a queer, somewhat Latin business, a little out of place to our English way of thinking.

* Make your choice of the three principal ways of saying, 'I'm awfully sorry but I like leg shows,' with careful reference to the character and personality of your opponent.

Countering and cross-countering in the more serious conversations reach extraordinary depths among advanced Lifemen. The ensuing notes are condensed from my Brochure.

HOW TO MAKE PEOPLE FEEL AWKWARD ABOUT RELIGION

The man who lets it be known that he is religious is in a strong life position. There is one basic rule. It is: Go one better. Fenn went too far. This is his method – in his own words:

To take the most ordinary instance – the simple Sunday churchgoer. 'Are you coming to church with us?' my host says. It is a little country church, and my host, Moulton, who has some claims to be a local squire, wants me to come, I know, because he is going to read the lesson. He reads it very well. He enjoys reading it. I heard him practising it to himself immediately after breakfast.

'Yes, why don't you come to church for once, you old sinner?' Mrs Moulton will say.

Do *not* mumble in reply to this: 'No, I'm afraid . . . I'm not awfully good at that sort of thing . . . my letters . . . catch post.'

On the contrary, deepen and intensify your voice, lay your hand on her shoulder, and say, 'Elsa' (calling her by her Christian name perhaps for the first time):

'Elsa, when the painted glass is scattered from the windows, and the roof is opened to the sky, and the ordinary simple flowers grow in the crevices of pew and transept – then and not till then will your church, as I believe, be fit for our worship.'

Not only does this reply completely silence opponent;

but it will be possible to go out and win ten shillings on the golf course, come back very slightly buzzed from Sunday pre-lunch drinks, and suggest, by your direct and untroubled look, before which their glance may actually shift, that by comparison with yourself your host and hostess, however innocently, have been only playing at religion.

That is Religious Basic. A harder character to tackle is the man of big personality with a grave, good-looking, rather biscuit-coloured face who digs himself in, so to speak, by being tremendously understanding and humorous, and by letting it be known that he belongs to a Group, and you needn't talk to him about it unless you feel like it.

The basic counter is, of course, to ask him about it almost before you have got into the room. Get him to explain, and after a few sentences say:

'Yes. Indeed I agree. I expect we all of us do. The only trouble is, it doesn't go far enough. In other words, it's not a religion. It's an ethic. And a religion is what we want. Now how many of us . . .' and then get going.

This works with the layman, but many an expert in Religionship is, in fact, an expert Lifeman of the first water.

If so he will seem to appreciate and indeed admire your answer and reply, 'Good. Good. Good. I'm not sure I don't rather agree.' Leaving you stuck with what we call the 'so what' diathesis.*

No. Deeds not words must be the rule in religious play. Take Jack Carraway. Effective enough in his way; but put him up against a real Lifeman like Brood or Offset or Odoreida and what happens?

---

* For 'diathesis' see O.K.-words (p. 28).

The Carraway Group believes in cheerfulness and helpfulness. Every morning Brood meets Carraway on the platform of Redhill station for the eight fifty. Every morning Brood says, 'Still sowing the seed, Carraway?' And the constant repetition of this joke, now for four

Fig. 3. Freehand drawing of Redhill Station from the North. The cross shows Platform 2, with Carraway's point of entrance.

hundred successive weekdays, is said, by Brood at any rate, to be imparting a one-sided effect to Carraway's smile.

Brutal methods against brutal men. Offset's plan was subtler. He used to catch Carraway's train at East Croydon, and whenever he happened to get into Carraway's carriage, Carraway would appal Offset by taking Offset's hand and helping him up the step, putting his bag on the rack for him, offering to 'swop papers' (which Offset was sometimes embarrassed to do owing to the nature of the paper he usually read), making room for him, and indeed, on two occasions, actually *giving up his seat*, telling Offset that he 'looked tired'.

But Offset soon developed an effective counter. Whenever Carraway showed signs of helping, quick as a knife he went one better. He kept sharpening pencils and giving them to Carraway, 'for the crossword', although in fact Carraway never did crosswords. He would be waiting at East Croydon with a large cup of absolutely boiling tea, an armful of magazines, and a piece of gingerbread, all for Carraway.

Arriving at London Bridge he would insist on helping

 him from the carriage, and on one occasion I saw Offset actually lift him out. It was on that occasion that we gave Offset the high place of 84 on our list of leading Lifemen.

Odoreida's method, if you can call it a method, was, of course, quite different and, if I must say so, typical of Odoreida. He not only allowed Carraway to help him in and to lift his usual small brown paper parcel on to the rack.

Fig. 4.
COUNTER RELI-
GIOUS PLAY. Offset
lifts down Carraway.

He actually sent him on errands for cigarettes or matches, got Carraway to give up his corner seat 'because of my train sickness', and usually borrowed five shillings because he had 'no change to tip the porter'.

NOTE ON O.K.-WORDS

My use of the word 'diathesis' reminds me that this is now on the O.K. list for conversationmen. We hope to publish, monthly, a list of words which may be brought in at any point in the conversation and used with effect because no one quite understands what they mean, albeit these words have been in use for a sufficiently long time, at any rate by Highbrowmen, say ten years, for your audience to have seen them once or twice and already felt uneasy about them.* We are glad to suggest two words for November:

Mystique

Classique

* I have often been asked whether there is an accredited counter for use against O.K.-words. Mrs Johnstone made a note of the following conversation between myself and J. Compton, the educationist (Lifeman 364). Compton used to do splendidly with the word 'empathy' when it was O.K. in the twenties, but we are none of us as young as we were. He was trying a fairly up-to-date O.K.-word which has been on our list since October 1938: 'Catalyst'.

COMPTON: I think Foxgrove acts as a useful catalyst to the eccentricities of his chairman.

SELF: Catalyst?

COMPTON: Yes.

SELF: Yes. I suppose 'catalyst' isn't *quite* right.

COMPTON (*surprised*): Not quite right?

SELF: Not quite what you mean. A catalyst is an agent of re-distribution, literally.

COMPTON: Oh, yes.

SELF: It is a re-alignment of the molecules rather than an alteration of their potential. . . .

COMPTON: In a sense . . .

Compton knows, and I know that he knows, that I am as ignorant of physics or chemistry as he is; yet nothing he can say will alter the general impression that in the feverish pursuit of the O.K.-word he has misfired with a metaphor, ployed by his own gambit.

2

LIFEMANSHIP PRIMORDIAL I

WEEK-ENDMANSHIP

The first lesson learnt, what better than to put that
lesson into practice with a will? You may already
have increased your chances of being one up on the
layman by fifty per cent. Where is this condition
more necessary to achieve than the social gathering
or week-end party? Yet, remember, that it is just on
such occasions as this that an appearance of geniality
is most important.

LET me, to start with, transcribe here a few notes, I
believe not unimportant, on the typical Week-endman –
based, I should add, on that grand Lifeman with that
fine old week-end name, G. Cogg-Willoughby.

What to record? I remember Cogg-Willoughby's first
action, coming down to supper – a late cold meal, on the
first night – the Friday night. The F. Meynells of Suffolk
live (he is of course the Gamesman) in a charmingly
appointed cottage,* but suffer, with one exception, from

* This cottage of the Meynells is in fact a beautifully altered
and luxurious Georgian house, but it is an *important general rule*
always to refer to your friend's country establishment as a 'cottage'. Why? Because it is an extraordinarily difficult gambit to
counter. Impossible to reply 'My *what*?' 'It's not really a cottage'
is no better if not worse.

T. Driberg, noted Essex Lifeman, himself possesses a beautifully
appointed and luxurious Georgian house, and, in the intervals of
concentrating on his great work *M.P.-manship*, promised for 1953,
he has done a good deal of work on Counter Cottaging, a sum-
mary of which he has sent us.

T. Driberg suggests that as answer to the generalized question an almost complete absence of staff. Immediately the meal was over, Cogg-Willoughby would take off his coat, roll up his sleeves, clear the table in a trice, and then, 'Let's get down to it,' he said, and would do all the washing-up, if not part of the drying-up as well, expertly and thoroughly, with a quick swish round even of one or two saucepans, and clean a cup, used at some previous meal with which he had no connexion. No need to add that, having planted this good impression in the mind of his hostess, 'Cogg' for the rest of the week-end would lift not one finger in the kitchen or the garden, nor bring in so much as a single log of firewood from the shed.

COGG-WILLOUGHBY AND ANTI-GAME PLAY

Cogg was in his element, as we well remember, at week-end parties where there were plenty of games to be played and plenty of people to play them. Incapable of any kind of sport, it was here that Cogg established his mastery.

While the rest of the guests were feebly organizing

'Are you going down to your cottage this week-end?' the reply should be a firm 'Yes,' followed after a small pause by one of the following 'phrases of extended qualification'. These should either refer (*a*) to the house, or (*b*) to the grounds.

(a) The House. (i) 'We've had to close the south wing altogether, except of course to the half-crown trippers.' (ii) 'I'm afraid Palladio didn't know much about the English climate! There's nothing like a classical colonnade to make the north wind whistle.' (iii) 'We're just having the octagon room done up. I wish I could get the Gainsboroughs back.' (iv) 'The man from the National Gallery has just been down to look at the Angelica Kauffmann mantelpiece.' (v) '*Nothing* takes so much dusting as a dome.'

(b) The Grounds. (i) 'The park looks lovely from the belvedere these summer mornings.' (ii) 'We have to keep an extra bailiff just to fill in forms.' (iii) 'I'm hoping to get some advice from Kew on restoring the maze.'

bowls, ping-pong, or cricket, Cogg would look on en-couragingly. Soon he would produce an enormous pair of field-glasses.

'Well, I'm going off for *my* game. See you all later. Sometimes it was bird-watching, sometimes butterflies, occasionally wild flowers. Cogg, of course, was almost

Fig. 5. Cogg-Willoughby at Ashton Broad Elm, graceful home of Lady Tilden, from a water-colour. The meaning of the lettering is uncertain. Note pediment, said to be the twelfth highest in East Anglia.

entirely ignorant of all these pursuits, but it was 99 to 1 the rest of the guests would know still less. Cogg would suddenly stand stock still. 'Listen,' he would say. Some feeble quack would be heard from the willow beyond the pond. 'That's an easy one to tell. The frog-pippit.' Then he would add, for a safety measure, 'as I believe they call it in these parts'.

By the Sunday most of the women guests would be following him round, standing stock still, in a trance, listening or looking at some bit of rubbish, while Cogg explained.

What I liked about Cogg was the cleanness and openness of his play. Only in one gambit did he seem to me to show a trace of unpleasantness, but I must say I was glad to see him employ it against that confirmed hostessnobbler, P. de Sint. In his specious, dark-haired way, de Sint was a typical hostess's favourite.

De Sint's first action at a summer week-end was always to strip to the waist and sun-bathe. Unlike Cogg (who remains white and slug-like) and myself (who quickly turn beetroot), de Sint will develop a rich honey bronze straight away.

Cogg was at his best in this situation. I have never more admired the easy coolness with which he dealt with a crisis. Late on the Sunday afternoon, it might be, he would look de Sint up and down. He would speak thoughtfully.

COGG-WILLOUGHBY: By Jove, you brown easily.

DE SINT: Do I?

COGG-WILLOUGHBY: Yes. You're one of the lucky ones.

DE SINT: Oh, I don't know.

COGG-WILLOUGHBY: They always say that the Southern types brown more easily.

DE SINT: Well, I don't know, I'm not particularly . . .

COGG-WILLOUGHBY: Oh, I don't know . . . Mediterranean . . .

Cogg-Willoughby was able to speak this phrase with an intonation which suggested that de Sint was of Italian blood at least, with, quite probably, a touch of the tar-

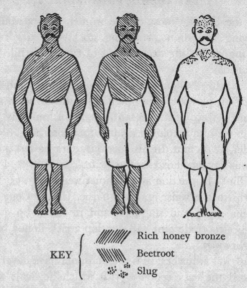

KEY	/////	Rich honey bronze
	\\\\\	Beetroot
	∴∴∴	Slug

Fig. 6. Types of sunburn. Students of week-endmanship should learn to distinguish these three 'sunburn results' at a glance.

brush in his ancestry as well. On three or four occasions, after this attack, I have noticed that de Sint spent the rest of the week-end trying to cover up every exposed inch of his body.

I do hope the reader will understand that I have only scratched the surface, in these notes, of week-endmanship; and that this account of Cogg-Willoughby, even, is far from complete.

THE ODOREIDA DIAGNOSIS

For basic week-end I should perhaps acknowledge, for once, the work of Odoreida.

Odoreida is usually incapable of pioneer work, but one

must admire his occasional flashes, such as this, reported to me (Odoreida in play against Redruth's Decline Gambit).

G. F. C. Redruth was basically a poor week-end man. With his tweedy skin, podgy legs, and boringly healthy cheeks, he looked like a fine Game Birdsman. But the fact is, he was an appallingly bad shot, and it was necessary for him to keep this fact concealed. In the old days, at the Blessinghams' when the Saturday morning shoot was being planned, 'Count me out of this,' he would say.

'Why?' (Mrs Blessingham – then Lady Blessingham – asked.)

'Not my cup of tea. Stupid old conscience at work. Don't like birds, but feel I wasn't created to take pot-shots at them. Besides, I think the creatures are rather beautiful.'

Odoreida, who always loathed Redruth, couldn't make much headway by murmuring, 'I suppose you miss them on purpose,' and when, in the evening, he said, 'I see you don't mind *eating* the beautiful creatures,' he was again put out by Redruth's technique of vaguely quoting the Bible.

'Let he who casts the first stone ...' said Redruth, and all this went down more than well with the Blessinghams, this being the time when they dropped their title *

---

* As most of you know, our Glasgow Group has been working for some time on snob and counter-snobship. The results are too uncoordinated to be included in this manual, but we have published from Yeovil a few promising first-fruits. Here is the list:

No. 8080   *Knights, and How to Reassure them about their Social Position.*

No. 71   *The Renunciation of Titles Bad Form: a Plea and a Counterblast.*

on conscientious grounds, and opened the grounds of their house and the annexe of the servants' quarters to the Basingstoke Liberal Summer School

But later, with General and Constance Ould, Redruth realized that Conscienceship was out of the question. Here, in order to conceal his feebleness with guns, Redruth used to suggest that, healthy though he looked superficially, it was dangerous for him to stand about even for a minute. The slightest hint of moving air on the skin, he was able to convey, might cause the old T.B. centres to become active again. It was good by-play on his part to be always wearing a hat, even indoors, if there was the faintest draught.

Odoreida, unable to stand this, countered by a method which none of us could have used, though we can but admire it. He was able to suggest, and indeed actually say, out of Redruth's hearing, of course, that the complaint Redruth actually suffered from was ringworm.

IMPORTANT PERSON PLAY

There is no doubt that basic week-endmanship should contain some reference to Important Person Play. It must appear that it is *you* who in mid-week life are the most important man. I always like to quote here the plucky ploying of poor Geoffrey Field. On the Friday evening he always seemed pretty done in. No question of having to entertain Field, or, indeed, of Field entertaining. He was there for a rest – had to be, got to be, if he was going to get through next week's work. He would

No. 38384 *Christian Names? Never!*

No. 31   *Famous People and When Not to Recognize Them.*

No. 491   *It's All Right Only Having an O.B.E.,* or *How to Avoid Full Dress; Six Easy Devices for the Undecorated.*

lie back, legs out, eyes relaxed, arms hanging straight down on the sides of the chair – content.* 'Sh – they

* It is extremely important to know if and when – and why – a Lifeman may put his feet up at the week-end party.

It suggests that you are important, it suggests that you are relaxed and at home in the house – a favoured guest. It suggests that you are tired. And it suggests another thing, too – that you are young.

Older men who wish to appear younger and have not been trained by us sometimes make the mistake of assuming a smart, energetic step, and generally bustling about. How wrong this is. To appear young, be slow and loose-limbed in your movements and put your feet up if possible over the *back* of the couch on which you are sitting. J. C. Jagger used to continue to do this even when well over fifty-eight and in agonies from neuritis.

It has been often asked: Did Jagger overdo this evolution? We believe, No: but overgambiting, at week-ends, can be a real danger.

CHILD PLAY, for instance (Beinggoodwithchildrenship), is, of course, of the utmost importance at many week-end parties, where your position as Top Man may depend on how you go down with your hostess's offspring.

We were never quite satisfied with the work of E. J. Workman, the author, in this field. [For the Workman approach, see under Writership, p. 66.] The Workman gambit is well-known enough. 'I talk to the child absolutely ordinarily,' he was constantly repeating, 'absolutely ordinarily, as if he was one of us. Absolutely ordinarily in the morning. Absolutely ordinarily at mealtimes,' said E.J.

It was before mealtimes, unfortunately, that Workman occasionally took one or two too many appetizers. I remember his turning to little Albert Groundhill, then aged five, and saying: 'Don't you agree? This endless physical exercise is a fetish?' Of course, Albert made no reply. Nor did small Judy Homer, aged six and a half, when after four rum and oranges E. J. asked her whether she 'didn't think, in some parts of England, people in villages were a good deal more immoral than people in towns. Whoopee.' This last was an unsuitable question for a child of six, or at any rate unsuitably put. Gambits are for use, not for overuse.

won't ring me up because (not a word) nobody knows where I am. Except Bales.'

No one knew who Bales was, and only I knew that he didn't exist, and that in fact Field had been out of a job for nine months. Yet there was a general tendency among the guests actually to wait on Field – tend him. At Liverpool Street on Monday morning Field used to say, 'Taxi? No thanks. The Ministry is sending or is alleged to be sending a car for me.'

When everybody had gone, Field would take a four-penny tube to Ealing Broadway, and play squash on the public courts, or rather knock up by himself.

3

LIFEMANSHIP PRIMORDIAL II

EXPERT MANAGEMENT

Do not hesitate, now that you have learnt some
simple rules, to use them. The thrill of the young
Lifeman, when he first puts his precepts into actual
practice! How to be one up on the expert – worthy
ploy. But this, too, is basic, since superior-knowledge
counter-play, the doing down of the specialist, is
primary whether life or Lifemanship is involved.
Indeed, my Bude audiences will remember that I
made this the first, not the third, of my lecture
series.

COUNTER EXPERT

I ALWAYS believe that some kind of ABC of counter
expert play is the best grounding for the young Lifeman.
Without any special knowledge, without indeed any
education whatever, it is possible not only to keep going
in conversation, but, sometimes, to throw grave doubts
on the value of expert knowledge in general.* There is no

---

* There is no need to stress the failure, here, of the sloppy expertship of the old school. The man who depended on mugging up
the subjects of his week-end fellow guests never went very far. The
classical example of this was, I always thought, G. Protheroe. On
one occasion, for instance, hearing that Dr Lowes, the expert on
Coleridge, was to be present during a week-end holiday, he spent
the previous month (he was a very slow reader) trying to memorize
the facts of a small, mass-produced life of S. T. Coleridge printed
in the These Men Have Made Their Mark series.

By the Sunday evening, when the visit was coming to an end, he
realized only too well that as yet *no reference to Coleridge had*

finer spectacle than the sight of a good Lifeman, so
ignorant that he can scarcely spell the simplest word,
making an expert look like a fool in his own subject, or at
any rate interrupting him in that stupefying *flow*, break-
ing the deadly *one upness* of the man who, say, has really
been to Russia, has genuinely taken a course in
psychiatry, has actually read history at Oxford, or has
written a book on something.

A few simple rules, then, for a start.

The Canterbury Block. We always encourage
youngsters to *practise as they learn.* Why not an easy
exercise to warm up? The expert on international rela-
tions is talking. He is in full spate. How can he be jolted?
(R. Bennett's variant.)

EXPERT: There can be no relationship based on a
   mutual dependency of neutral markets. Otto Hüsch
   would not have allowed that. He was in Vienna at the
   time. . . .
LIFEMAN (*as if explaining to the rest of the audience*):
   It was Hüsch who prevented the Archbishop from
   taking office in Sofia.

A suggestion only. But no matter how wild Lifeman's

been made. During a pause in the conversation he decided to
speak.
PROTHEROE: I am right in saying, I believe, that there are two
   versions of the 'Ancient Mariner', and they are not the same.
LOWES: 1798 and 1800?
PROTHEROE: 1798 and 1800. . . .
LOWES: Yes – they are not the same.
PROTHEROE: Not the same.
   And here the conversation ended. Easy to find fault with Pro-
theroe. Not so easy to formulate the basic rules which turn failure
into success.

quiet insertion may be, it is enough to create a pause, even a tiny sensation.

Nor is the typical Block necessarily complex. The beauty of the best Canterbury is its deadly simplicity, in the hands of an expert. Six words will suffice.

EXPERT (*who has just come back from a fortnight in Florence*): And I was glad to see with my own eyes that this Left-wing Catholicism is definitely on the increase in Tuscany.

THE CANTERBURY: Yes, but not in the South.*

'Yes, but not in the South,' with slight adjustments, will do for any argument about any place, if not about any person. It is an impossible comment to answer. And for maximum irritation, remember, the tone of voice must be 'plonking'.

Here, then, we have two forms of what is known as the Canterbury Block.† For 'plonking', see next paragraph.

WHAT IS PLONKING?

If you have nothing to say, or rather, something extremely stupid and obvious, say it, but in a 'plonking' tone of voice – i.e. roundly, but hollowly and dogmatically. It is possible, for instance, to take up and repeat with slight variation, in this tone of voice, the last phrase of the speaker. Thus:

TYPOGRAPHY EXPERT: ... and roman lower-case letters of Scotch and Baskerville have two or three thou.

---

* I am required to state that World Copyright of this phrase is owned by its brilliant originator, Mr Pound (see Fig. 7).

† This word has nothing to do with Block; nor has Canterbury with Canterbury. The phrase is good 'White Celtic' and almost certainly derives from Kan-tiubh bribl-loch (literally the 'war-winning man-of-words' in the 'porcelain-expert foray').

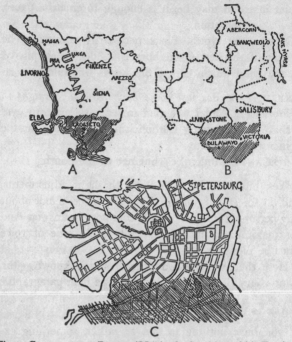

Fig. 7. CANTERBURY BLOCK ('Not in the South' gambit). To give
added effect to this phrase, some Lifemen carry a small packet of a
dozen districts chosen at random with the southern area shaded.
Tuscany (*a*), Rhodesia (*b*), and St Petersburg (*c*) are suitable.

more *breadth*, which gives a more generous tone, an
easier and more spacious colour, to the full page –
YOURSELF: The letters 'have width'.
T. E.: Exactly, exactly, exactly – and then if –
YOURSELF: It is a widening.
T. E.: What? – Oh yes, yes.

This is the lightest of trips, yet, if properly managed,
the tone of voice will suggest that you can afford to say

the obvious thing, because you have approached your conclusion the hard way, through a long apprenticeship of study.

'Plonking' of a kind can be made by the right use of quotation or pretended quotation. (See under Conversationship, p. 21.) Here is the rough format:

MILITARY EXPERT (*beginning to get into his stride, and talking now really well*): There is, of course, no precise common denominator between the type of mind which, in matters of military science, thinks tactically, and the man who is just an ordinary pugnacious devil with a bit of battlefield instinct about him.

YOURSELF (*quietly plonking*): Yes, ...* 'Where equal mind and contest equal go.'

This is correct quotation plonking (*a*) because it is not a genuine quotation and (*b*) because it is meaningless. The Military Expert must either pass it over, smile vaguely, say 'yes,' or in the last resort, 'I don't quite get ...' In any case, it *stops flow*, and suggests that whatever he is saying, you have got there first.

I WAS NEVER IN VLADIVOSTOCK

These early gambits mastered, the student can begin his study of more advanced expertship. Here is a slightly more complex ploy against the man, always dangerous, who has actually been there.

This expert can only be attacked on his own ground. And the basis of attack is to take if possible *one foreign place* where you have *actually been*. A convenient one for young British Draftees who have spent their army

* For the vocal equivalent of the printed dot, see my early pamphlet, *Whither BBCmanship?*

year in Germany is Munster Lager, transit and demobilization camp, well known to them, but entirely unknown to anybody over the age of twenty-one. Munster Lager is good, because it can be pronounced, by variation, as if it was a placename of any country. The conversation goes like this. Subject, say, Fishing Rights on Russia's Eastern Seaboard. The expert coming in to the attack:

TRAVEL EXPERT: Well, I don't know, but when I was in Vladivostock, I knew there was going to be trouble. Nyelinsky was on the warpath even then, and I was fortunate enough to meet his staff with the Korean Councillor.

AUDIENCE: Really?

TRAVEL EXPERT: The local papers were front-paging it day after day. I soon *sensed* a very nasty situation, even if it didn't blow up then. It wasn't a very *comfortable* visit, but I was glad I'd been, afterwards.

SELF: Yes.

TRAVEL EXPERT: You see —

SELF: I was going to say — I'm sorry.

TRAVEL EXPERT: I'm sorry?

SELF: I was going to say that though I was never in Vladivostock, I *did* spend some months in Munster Lager, not a million miles away. (*The pronunciation can be slurred into something like Man Stalagin.*)

TRAVEL EXPERT: Oh, yes?

SELF: Of course, I was working as a stevedore among the dockers and porters ... I didn't see much of the high-ups, I'm afraid. But, Lord, I feel I understood the *people* — the cutters and the quay-cleaners, the doss-men and the workers on the factory fringe. The wives waiting on the quayside, waiting with their children. I needn't say where my sympathies lay.

Often the Travel Expert is completely shut up by this kind of talk; but it is *not for beginners*. The clever Lifeman can continue in this vein indefinitely, without ever having to say, or not, that he has been in Asia, or that, in fact, he has not.

GO ON TALKING

A very small probe, which yet is not ineffective, has been used by Cogg-Willoughby, who has been fairly successful with a series of counterings from the psychiatrist's angle.

The expert holds the floor. His audience is submissive. Cogg waits, attentive. Sooner or later the expert will say, 'But I'm talking too much' – always a prelude to talking still more. Or, 'What do you think,' he may even say, simply.

EXPERT: But you say. What do you think?

COGG-WILLOUGHBY: No, go on.

EXPERT: But I have been going on!

COGG-WILLOUGHBY: I know. But it's good. It's right. I knew as soon as I came in you were happy. You – you look so natural. . . .

EXPERT: Natural?

COGG-WILLOUGHBY: Yes, it's all right: don't take any notice of what I say. It's good.

EXPERT: Good?

COGG-WILLOUGHBY: It means that you're what we call happy. Go ahead. We're all listening to you.

Cogg was extraordinarily successful with this sequence for a time, and it led him to explore, curiously enough, the field of counter psychiatry. Cogg's Anti Psyke, as it came to be called, is not well known, and I have been asked to publish a note on it here. He had two principal tactics, and trained himself to make a spontaneous choice of either.

Tactic One, his favourite, was used against direct attack by an accredited psycho-analyst. This would be the shape of the dialogue – or at any rate these were the words I noted down when he was set against Krautz Ebenfeld. Imagine, if you can, the thick Slovenic accent of the one and the quiet Cambridge tones of Cogg for contrast:

COGG: I expect you are always observing and analysing, Dr Ebenfeld.

EBENFELD: It is my job.

COGG: You will make me self-conscious.

EBENFELD: Why is that? It is what you do when you are not conscious that interests me. Do you know that you caress the back of your neck with your left hand when you speak to me?

COGG (*who has been doing this on purpose*): No. Really?

EBENFELD: Do you know why that is?

COGG: Well – you mean ...

EBENFELD: You had a brother or a young cousin who was a fine swimmer, yes?

COGG: Rather!

EBENFELD: And you perhaps were not much of a swimmer. Yes?

COGG (*very warmly*): How glad I am to hear you say that.

EBENFELD: Glad?

COGG: The doctrine of '95, supported by you of all people.

EBENFELD: Ninety-five what?

COGG: Back to the founder of all founders – and how

rightly. Hardt's doctrine, as my own father taught it
to me.

EBENFELD: Yes – Hardt ...

COGG: How well did Freud say, in his queer English,
'He is my look up to. I stand to him – pupil.'

'That is very interesting,' says Ebenfeld. But he realized
he was gambited. Later Cogg even reduced Sophie Har-
mon, the great lay psychiatrist, to silence.

In this case (*Tactic Two*) Sophie as usual began it.

SOPHIE: You have a limp?

COGG: No.

SOPHIE: You were dragging your foot as you crossed the
room.

COGG (*smelling a rat*): Was I?

SOPHIE: You are not satisfied, fulfilled, today?

COGG: Ah.

SOPHIE: You have *two motives* pulling different ways.

COGG: My limp, you mean?

SOPHIE: Perhaps.

COGG (*lowering his voice yet speaking more distinctly*):
Perhaps. Or just an old weakness of the paradel-
toid?

SOPHIE: Perhaps.

Sophie keeps her head, but she is ployed, and Cogg
knows it, knowing that she never took anatomy.

It is easy to bungle Counter Psychiatry, which is, of
course, a huge subject (see end of this chapter). But it is
essential, we now believe, to work at these opening exercises before the more intricate problems are attempted
– before dealing, that is to say, with the experts in paint-
ing and music, politics and philosophy.

To murmur 'exhibitionist' or 'Oedipus' or just to whisper the one word 'aunt' when any rival is in full flow is a fine ploy, equalling Lifemanship at its best.

NOTE. For 'incest' read 'aunt' throughout.

THE LIFEMANSHIP PSYCHO-SYNTHESIS CLINIC

Lifemen have not been backward in the counter-attack: and those of us whose job it is to deal with this kind of thing possess, as some readers know, a certain top floor room not a hundred miles from Wimpole Street where we are setting up

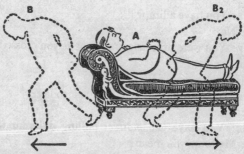

Fig. 8. PSYCHO-SYNTHESIS IN WELBECK STREET (diagram). Note the couch, which can be easily adapted from the old psycho-analyst's couch or *tentade*. The 'psycho' himself (A), is, of course, the reclining figure. The patient is, or should be, striding from B to B2 and, of course, back.

our school – openly lay – of psycho-synthesis. LET US RESTORE YOUR INHIBITIONS is our phrase. SUBLIMATE WITH US. We can put back the Hamlet into YOU.

Our workers in Wimpole Street make it perfectly clear that they are not qualified physicians. That they are not recognized by the Medical Council. That they are unattached to any hospital or clinic. We do not prescribe. We do not even advise. All we want you to do is to talk, and talk guardedly. Never mention the first thing that comes into your head. It will seem strange at first to the old-fashioned patient to find the psycho-synthesist lying relaxed on the couch while he the patient will be encouraged to walk up and down feverishly. You are suffering from a suppressed and thwarted conscious. Give intellectual self-criticism free rein.

A charge of a few guineas is made for each visit. The first treatment is bi-weekly for six months. At the end of this period it is normal and natural to hate, and indeed loathe, your synthesist. This is a sign that the thing is working, but that the treatment should continue until the patient gets out of the Dislike Phase.

The natural antagonists of all Lifemen, or shall I call them 'friendly enemies' of the lifeplay, are the psycho-analysts. They have their own organization, their own literature, their own terminology. Lifemen have always recognized the value of their 'psycho-analytic look' for stopping conversation. Now Lifemen have a chance to hit back.

SUPPORT LIFEMANSHIP BY JOINING

A LIFEMANSHIP ORGANIZATION

(All fees and subscriptions are sent direct to Station Road, Yeovil)

THE LIFEMANSHIP PSYCHO-SYNTHESIS CLINIC

4

WI' DOWNCAS' HEID

SOME NOTES ON CONTEMPORARY WOOMANSHIP
We publish these Notes not without some pride, as
they are the first fruits of our first Research Gala, as
we call it. It is interesting that twelve times as many
workers volunteered to send in reports on Woomanship as on any other subject. Looking round at a
group of our lads, I think we could say that our
features are essentially kind and wholesome-looking,
even if we have not got the regular profiles of a
haberdasher's advertisement. Still, be we who we
may, I am sorry I have space here to include so few
of our experiments, most of which, though not uni-
formly successful, show, I believe it will be agreed,
spirit.

HISTORY

VOLUMES will be written about the historical aspects of
that huge sub-department of Lifemanship, Woomanship.
It was known, certainly, in early China. The Cretans were
said to woo and 'enjoy patterns of woo behaviour' before
becoming engaged to each other.

May I say here that the question whether or not woomanship should be taught in schools has been answered
by me in the affirmative? It is rational, it is perfectly all
right, it has great beauty, treated in the proper way; in
fact, there is really nothing in it. At any rate, the go-
ahead headmaster of the Pennine Grammar School
smiled on the class in this subject which I held for his
charges.

My task now is to collect reports on some of the leading Woomen and Woo-women of today. I have a sheaf of them in my hand now for tabulation and collation. But wooing is, of course, a very human subject and many aspects of it are readily understandable to the general public.

WOO BASIC

'... for each approach, the method. ...'

THROUGH THE GEARS WITH GATTLING-FENN

Each woman presents a different problem, or, alternatively, each woman presents the same problem. How often that has been said. To that sound old Wooman Gattling-Fenn, the problem, and the approach, was always the same, a fact or situation which may owe its being to Gattling-Fenn's undoubted limitations. He was getting bald in a curious way. Yet he was always falling in love with horrifyingly pretty girls of vacant minds.

To see Gattling-Fenn at work on one such is to see woo basic at its best. There is nothing new about the theory of Gattling's 'gradually-awakened-interest' approach. But his practice of it has never been improved upon.

'The rule', he was always telling us, 'is not so much to seem to be attracted against your will, as to give the impression that you can scarcely bring yourself to speak to her. And this in spite of the fact, you are at the same time able to indicate, that the face you are addressing happens by some racial fluke, some luck of the ethnological draw, of some genetical jackpot, to be as near the perfection of sexual beauty as mortal may be.'

Gattling-Fenn used often to talk in fairly long words. It was part of his method. But he also talked in short words, too; and in the opening stages he was monosyllabic.

Gattling, having succeeded by much pushing and side-stepping in planting himself next to some mentally feeble girl, begins as follows: *

G.-F. (*struggling against boredom*): I have, in fact, seen you before. Being important in some film shot. Denham, Stage II.

The girl will be unlikely to deny absolutely that she has even been in a film studio, but will probably say:

GIRL: Oh – I don't think so.
G.-F.: Sorry, a bad professional blob of mine.
GIRL: Professional?
G.-F.: Yes, I'm sorry. There was one period of my life, I'm sorry to say, when it was my job to stare at Film Faces.

At this moment he suddenly wrenches his glasses out of his pocket, rams them on his nose, stares, and snatches them off again. (See Spectacles, management of.)

GIRL: Oh?
G.-F.: Selecting the perfect film profile – one of J. Arthur's more surprisingly imaginative ideas. Two hundred and fifty dead straight noses. Two hundred and fifty pairs of brilliant eyes, oh so large and liquid. I'm afraid you're rather the type.
GIRL: Were you really?
G.-F.: How do you mean?

* The principle of Instantaneous Speech is important. No good, if you get into a railway carriage solely occupied by some woo-worthy girl, waiting for half an hour and offering her a cigarette at about Reading, after premonitory mumbles and throat-clearing. Gattling always used to maintain that he would start speaking to the girl while still half in the corridor, saying, for instance (if she is reading *The Times*), 'Good heavens, I thought *The Times* had ceased publication,' naturally and easily, as he entered.

GIRL: I mean, what did you have to do?

G.-F.: Me? Just be the final judge and take the unfor-
tunate creature to various functions. You don't act at
all, do you? I have an office job at the moment, and I'm
wondering whether even the theatre isn't better than
that. I'm no good at being a ten till five man.

GIRL: Oh, *I* have to be at the office at nine.

FIRST GEAR

This, of course, is the moment to slip in Gear One.
Gattling leans forward fractionally, and although he has
in fact been staring at the girl all the evening he manages
to give the impression that he is seeing her, now, for the
first time.

G.-F.: What – you have a job?

GIRL: Oh yes.

G.-F.: I mean a real human job, doing things, working,
like myself – with all the routine, and sometimes the
thrill? How wise of you – to be part of the pattern. You
mix with people. Know people.

GIRL: Oh, you see a lot of people. I don't think it'd
interest you much.

Gears Two and Three should follow automatically.*

NOTE. Gattling-Fenn's 'Period of Indifference' is not to be
confused with the phase, or sub-phase, known as The Imper-
sonal Love-letters of Allchick. This was the ploy, now in

---

* According to Gattling. But the truth is he was never very
successful. He told me once that he only took up this particular
approach because his Dog Gambit had failed so completely. In the
old days he used to approach a girl with a dog, and establish
affinity by showing his fondness for these pets. 'How's Wog-Wog,'
he would say, speaking solely *to the animal*. But latterly, owing to
the bizarre appearance of Gattling's hair, all dogs growled with
real menace at the first sound of his voice.

frequent use, of T. Allchick, who in the midst of the wildest and most tempestuous love affair would write letters to the girl beginning 'Dear Madeleine', continue for a few lines on the theme 'my cold is very much better', and end up 'Yours cordially'. I remember the original Madeleine well, and these letters certainly added fuel to the flames of her love for T. Allchick. Why it worked is a mystery. Allchick's American imitator, B. Benedict Hume, used to sign himself 'Yours spontaneously'. There are many who believe in the extremely ardent love-letter, twelve pages long : but there is certainly a case against them.

WOOMANSHIP SECONDARY

BEING ONE THING OR THE OTHER, OR, ALTERNATIVELY, BEING ONE THING AND THEN THE OTHER

Most of the experts agree here. The sound wooman is either fascinatingly rich or amusingly poor. It is bad gambiting to have a normal income.

Similarly, he must either be charmingly weak about women, feckless, and extravagant; or he must be slow to move, stolid, and dependably waiting for the 'One Woman'.

Similarly, one must either be the experienced ladies' man, with correct Flower Play; or alternatively, one must be so gauche as to be the kind of man who has never given a bunch of flowers in his life, doesn't know where to buy them, and waits till the taxi has been chugging back to Hammersmith for twenty minutes before he breaks the silence by saying 'Can I kiss you?'

In the same way, the wooman must ask himself: Is he going to be vague so as to get the 'He's so vague, let me look after him without his knowing it' reaction? Or is he going to be quietly definite, precise, and well-ordered, so as to make use of the 'I can depend on him' diathesis.*

THE WILKES METHOD

On the physical side it is most important, finally, to decide whether you are (*a*) handsome, or (*b*) ugly. The ugly man, or the half-and-half who decides to be ugly, must learn to suggest, like Wilkes, that though the ugliest man in the country, yet, given half an hour's start of the handsomest man in Britain, he could out-woo him with any girl he liked. Of recent years, P. Wilkes has done well with this. He will get himself introduced to the girl, stare crossly at the floor, and then say suddenly:

WILKES: I'm sorry. I don't seem to have anything to say as usual.

GIRL: Oh, well, it's stupid to talk all the time, isn't it?

WILKES: I was trying to put myself in your place, while I was trying – forgive me – not to stare at your face. You see ... you have this marvellous lookability – this ability, by your face alone, to thaw.

* It is sometimes necessary to combine both of any two opposed approaches, or rapidly substitute one for another, if the first isn't working. Have you decided that the *dependable* line is not succeeding? Do you wish to seem uncared for and in need of a woman's touch? BILLINGTON'S WOO AIDS LTD supply special Esioff imitation inkstains, a file for fraying cuffs, a pair of 'Break-Phast' shoelaces and their useful 'Odsox' for the man who wants, in a hurry, to look carelessly dressed. (See Fig. 9.) All profits are sent direct to Station Road, Yeovil. HELP LIFEMANSHIP.

Fig. 9. 'Odsox' brand of odd socks for suggesting that wooman suffers from neglect of his home life. (Billington's Woo Aids Ltd)

GIRL: Thaw?

WILKES: To melt – melt the resistance of making con
tact which is in all of us. Whereas. in my case, there
is this barrier of my pretty fearsome countenance. I
think –

GIRL (*looking at him*): But, I don't know –

WILKES: I know what you're going to say. You have got
an essential delicious kindness –

GIRL: I think you've got rather a nice face.* Sort of.†

---

* Wilkes had, in fact, a rather well-shaped and expressive left
cheek, with interesting lines and dents in it, deepened by repeated
exercises, including the turning on and off of bath taps with his
teeth, which he did for five minutes every morning. He would at
this point in the above conversation affect an expression of humorous scepticism, lay a special smile (exercise 2) on the left side of
his face only, at the same time moving his head underneath a top
light, to give a deep-set effect to his eyes. (See Fig. 10 on opposite
page.)

† B. Boak, in spite of his unfitting name, decided that it was
more suitable to him to be not ugly but the reverse, handsome.

This made little difference to Boak's general manner, except that
he would from time to time stand stock-still, saying to himself ten
times over 'I am handsome, I am handsome', until he had con-
vinced himself that some girl he was after had been struck by
'the immobility of his features'. The fact that for Boak this gambit was never known to work does nothing to disprove the general
soundness of the approach.

It was rather amusing to see Boak at work on the same girl in
opposition to Victor Weiss. Weiss preferred the approach from
ugliness, and while Boak stood about like a statue saying to himself 'The remorseless precision of my profile,' Weiss would pace
huntedly up and down in the 'I am an outcast from the world of
beauty' stage of his attack.

No progress was ever made, in fact, on either side, because the
features of both were only remarkable for their complete ordinari-
ness – indeed it was impossible to remember Weiss's face for two
minutes consecutively.

THE STAINES METHOD

The necessity of having to be very much one thing or the other oppresses some novice or diffident woomen. They have to decide when making basic plans whether, say, to be a Leonardo (intellectual all-rounder), a Fry (games all-rounder), or just a plain attentive man-in-the-background who 'refuses to do anything unless he can do it perfectly'.

But remember that William Staines elaborated a method by which by concentrating on *one part*, he was able to suggest *the whole*.

Staines's particular approach was to establish himself

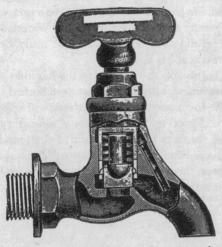

Fig. 10. TAP recommended for graded mouth exercises. Its simple shape and wide, flat flanges are adapted for gripping with teeth. Supplied by R. & J. Hart, 69 Cumberland House, Penge. (See first footnote on opposite page.)

as the 'perfect ladies' man with exquisite manners and real consideration'. Yet anybody who knew anything about Staines when he was off gambit knew that he was slothful, dirty, bad mannered, and had never, off gambit or on, opened a door for a lady in his life. Yet by concentrating on one tiny department of chivalry he somehow captured the whole.

He had a rack of a dozen lighters, which he cleaned and put in order once a week. Before making for his girl, he would select one, fuel it, put in a new flint, taking care to choose a large and manly one for the tiny, frightened girl, or one, for instance, with cigarette case and pencil attached for the slightly oopsy girl. At precisely the right moment in the cigarette manoeuvre, fire would dart from his hand. He had trained himself to see a pretty girl feel for a cigarette across three platforms of Waterloo Station, as it were, and to be behind her, flame ready, before the cigarette was at her lips.

The beauty of the Staines method is that once his gentlemanliness with lighters was established, the girl would be so stunned with the perfection of this particular piece of good manners that she would never question his good manners in general, even if she found herself left with the two heaviest bags to carry, and was asked to stand over them while Staines himself went into the refreshment room for a cup of tea.

BOY-PLAY

This sacred and ancient woo basic is too well-known and general to need more than a footnote or two in a modern work. The conception of boy-play arose as a reaction against knightly chivalry and romance, an alleviation of the general boredom women were feeling for the knightly gambit, a rebellion first noted at the time of the Third Crusade.*

Remember that though the essence of the boymanship gambit is a boy-like gaucherie and enthusiastic barging in, it is not necessary to be an actual boy to practise it, as officially it is part of standard woomanship up to the age of fifty-six: and G. Hollins of Oakwell Park still makes his mark with it at the age of seventy-seven, with no sign of fading success to date (I am writing in September 1950).

MORTON'S FOLLY

General rules themselves often go agley in the application. There is the case, for instance, of D. Morton. His method was a variety of the Gattling-Fenn. He would imply to the girl that, frankly, a certain type of woman was inclined to fall for him, suggesting, of course, that a succession of piercingly beautiful girls were for ever hammering at his door.

No man worked harder at this ploy than Morton. If, by a kind of trick, he did succeed in persuading by the promise of some job or other a really thunderously beautiful girl to go out with him, he would say, 'Look, do you mind if we go into the Six Hundred first, for a drink?' After that, 'I think we might pop across the road to the Avenue Bar. Billy Goatridge might be around.' Morton would then rush the tiring girl round six or seven bars and clubs in the hope of seeing at least one woman he wanted to impress, and demonstrate to them the extraordinary beauty of the women who, like the one he

* See Trevelyan's *Social History of England*, p. 126, paragraph beginning: 'It was no wonder, after seven years of minstrelsy, foreign travels "in her service", and a red rose bunged into the casement window once a month, that some of the women were beginning to get most frightfully fed up.'

was with, he would explain afterwards, insisted on his keeping an old birthday date with him'.*

'CIGARETTE STUBS OF JARVIS'

Students are often agley when they are asked to describe the meaning of this phrase. The correct answer to 'What is meant by "the Cigarette Stubs of Jarvis"?' is as follows:

(1) It is a ploy in woomanship.

(2) It was devised, as a variant of Mortonism, by J. Jarvis of Parkstone.

(3) Its object is to impress by suggesting that the wooer enjoys acquaintanceship with several other smart and sophisticated girls.

(4) It needs for its performance (*a*) a car with (*b*) a pull-out ash-tray built into the front of the panel (the 'LUV-MATCH' ash-tray, designed by Jarvis himself, is supplied). (All proceeds to Station Road, Yeovil.)

* D. Morton's younger brother, O., used his own variant of the above. He knew three well-known writers whom he had managed to induce to call him by his Christian name. He would bring a handsome girl to meet these people. A girl like Ethel Baird, for instance, who had read three novels of Dickens and had been to the Old Vic. He would introduce her to these literary friends one at a time or together, telling them 'she admires your work'.

Soon Ethel would be getting on with these personalities well enough, but Morton's object, to show this girl his familiarity with the great, was always defeated. His Christian name happened to be the rather curious one of Orlando, and though he really knew J. B. Priestley quite well and called him 'Jack', Priestley, naturally, could never bring himself to say 'Hallo, Orlando,' when other people were present.

The fact may now be admitted, since they have retired from Lifemanship, that the Mortons never had the necessary drive and gusto for this gambit or its derivatives. Both were handicapped by an almost complete absence of chin. A simpler and more radical approach should somehow have been devised for them.

(5) Jarvis's procedure was as follows: He filled the ash-tray with cigarette stubs. He then bought half a dozen lipsticks in striking but contrasted reds (Fatal Apple, Eden End, Oblivion, Cinderella's Pumpkin, Lovers' Lip,

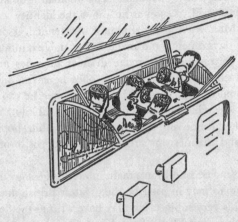

Fig. 11. The original ashtray used by Jarvis in his 'cigarette stub' gambit. The side is made transparent, semi-diagrammatically, to show the position of cigarette stubs normally hidden from view. Let the children get to work with crayons or water-colours to suggest the contrasted lipstick tints.

etc.) and painted the ends of the stubs with these reds to give an impression not only of the smartness, but of the variety and frequency of his companionship with other girls.

NOTE. Few, if any, women liked this gambit, but it impressed his fellow-woomen in the Cromer (Norfolk) area.

TRIANGULATION, OR THIRD PERSON PLAY

To prove, if proof were necessary, that approaches must

be varied, it is only necessary to consider for a moment the essential Woo Situation.

The very word 'woo' suggests an unwillingness on the part of the object: and that, carried one step further, means a previous attachment.* The wooman if he knows his business will, as soon as he knows the identity of this Second Man, leave the girl almost unattended, if necessary for days on end, and make a thorough examination of this person, observe, make discreet inquiries at his place of employment. And then, once he is thoroughly acquainted with the Second Man's character, he can woo with a clear mind and high heart. For he will know what to do. He must be sure that his character, habits, hobbies, tastes, and mannerisms are the precise opposite of his rival's.

Supposing Second Man's main interest is geology. Now the wooman may himself be the greatest British authority on this very subject. He may have written the definitive work on the Flora of the Upper Cretaceous. But he mustn't reveal it for a second. Keep geology dark, and particularly fossils.

In other words, the wooman must in all respects *be the opposite* of this Second Man, whose preserve, so far from being a hindrance, may in this way be actually turned to advantage.

'I'm not quite sure that I shall *ever* understand how the North Downs and the South Downs are part of a denuded anticlyne,' says this thoughtful girl the first time she dines out with wooman. 'I don't even know exactly

---

* From time to time woomen report painful examples of attachments which are fixed. This is itself the gambit of Darby and Joanmanship, and includes Still-ridiculously-in-love-with-each othering. Strong gambit as it may be, it is opposed, essentially, to the spirit of Lifemanship.

where the North Downs and the South Downs are,' says the wooman. She makes no reply, but her eyes grow a shade softer.

WILDWORTHY'S COUNTER TO THE CUNNINGHAM INDIFFERENCE

A pretty example of Third Person Play arose originally as a counter to the sound Indifference Play of Cunningham.

E. D. C. Wildworthy, of the Board of Trade, fell in love, from a distance, with Ivy Spring. Cunningham was Second Man, and had been doing well with Ivy through his amazing indifference to everything she did. Whether Ivy appeared in a new hat, an old hat, or an old dress

Fig. 12. Wildworthy's Counter to the Cunningham Indifference. Note that normal relative position of radio set and piano is reversed. The radio is usually *on top* of piano.

brilliantly renovated and cut in half, Cunningham would never notice the difference, but would always greet her in precisely the same way, 'Well, here we are again.'

Ivy, who had been brought up to 'keep her man on the alert' so as not to let him be too sure of what she was like, doubled and redoubled her efforts to attract his curiosity – I remember on one occasion, for instance, she turned up for a date with Cunningham with a Yale undergraduate in American sporting clothes on each arm, she herself wearing the uniform of a lance bombardier. 'Well,' said Cunningham, when he turned up, a little late, 'here we are again.'

This fascinated Ivy at first, of course, as it was bound to do. But actually from the woo point of view, I realized that Cunningham was dangerously liable to be third-personed; and when E. D. C. Wildworthy began to lay plans for Ivy, I watched with interest. He already knew Cunningham. His right procedure was obvious. The danger was, of course, that he might make it obvious to Ivy – as a procedure. He might notice and appreciate every time Ivy remembered to wind up her wrist-watch.

In the end he hit the mark by means of a simple trick. Arriving early one evening at Ivy's flat, while she was shouting at him through the door to make himself a drink, what in fact he did was to take the radio set, which usually rested on the piano, and reverse the positions, so that the piano rested on the radio set. When Ivy came in he said:

'What a good idea to change those round. It breaks the line of the room *much* better. You really *are* rather a clever girl.' Ivy, of course, couldn't remember having touched them, thought she must have done it in her sleep, but wasn't going to let on that it was luck not cunning. At the same time, she said to herself at once, This is the man for me.*

* Is this the place to point out that there are many woomen who hold that the above gambits are too complicated if not unnecessary and that there are those who believe that it is possible to make love successfully without having read this chapter? A group of Derbyshire Lifemen have done well among woo gambiters by going about with simple straightforward expressions and happy looks, suggesting that for them the hectic ploying of the average wooman is unnecessary. 'I am in love,' their silence seems to suggest, 'and the girl is in love with me.'

Odoreida has a counter of sorts to this counter. 'Well,' he will say to some poised-looking wooman in execution of this 'I have found her' gambit — 'Well, how is your little caper with Julia going?'

This is quite effective.

5

WRITERSHIP

Authorship consists very largely of a succession of enormous gambits. Wordsworth is obviously one big ploy. So are Macaulay, Prudence Wheeler, and a hundred others. The boundary between these and our own work in this field is often a very narrow one. However, the Yeovil Trustees have agreed, perhaps artificially, to demarcate the following ploys as genuine ploys of writership.

BASIC WRITERSHIP

WE will take Workman as a sound example of the basic writerman.

The novels of E. J. Workman were of the third class in respectable fiction. He never sold less than 15,000; usually 25,000.

He never trained with us, but it was on our advice that he changed his name. His real name, Cyril Delamere, was much too near the truth to be used in his particular author ploy.

He lived at a sufficiently inconvenient distance from the furthest flung station of Metroland to be regarded as a countryman, in a modernized house one wall of which, after tremendous hacking and scraping, stood revealed as genuine Georgian.

He wore an open-necked flannel shirt in the morning; on country walks usually had a large sheepdog at his heels, though he obviously disliked dogs and knew nothing of sheep; made regular visits to the private bar of his local and played a great deal of darts very badly, got *Picture Post* to photograph him in the ancient bowl-ing alley of the 'Feathers' over the caption 'E. J. ROLLS A PRETTY PUMPKIN WITH THE LANDLORD'. In order to look more like a country author he would screw a camp-stool into uncomfortable but sheltered little corners of his garden, in order to acquire sunburn while writing, well aware that he burnt very slowly and patchily. He would also talk extremely ordinarily to everyone; if possible most ordinarily to some wandering gypsy, noted village crook, or village sex maniac – so ordinarily, in fact, that they scarcely knew what he was getting at. He would also talk equally ordinarily to the rector and the local titled woman. He was extremely ordinary about cricket and infected everybody in the team with an unusually ordin-ary way of hanging about the pavilion.

If anybody asked him some important literary question – the meaning of a word or the place of a preposition – he would say, 'Yes, what the hell is the correct thing there?' as ordinarily as anybody.

Occasionally, with him in the 'Feathers' on Saturday nights, I would see him take in a week-end guest, with business-like face, neat town suit and glistening black hair. This unsuitable man would be made to drink pints of beer and play darts till long after closing time. 'Film executive,' I said to myself. For E. J. Workman would in fact introduce these men with a 'got to be careful of him ... I'm absolutely hopeless at the money side ... he understands it all, anyway'.

But I felt sorry for this stranger because I knew that he was probably negotiating for the film rights of one of the Workman novels, and that if so one could be certain that going home after his exhausting time in this Bucks re-treat he would find himself £1,200 down on the deal. For though E. J. Workman couldn't write, he was ferociously bright on the finance side, had been his own agent with brilliant success for twenty-five years, and had made the acquisition of almost criminally favourable film contracts his special hobby.

About the middle of August, when the carefully acquired red on Workman's forehead was beginning to turn a colour which might conceivably be called brown, Workman would start complaining of the endless drudge of the farmer's life. Workman had three 1,000-acre farms, each separately run by a first-class bailiff and a large staff, the whole ably coordinated by Workman when he met his bailiffs, whom he called by their Christian names, for half an hour on Saturday mornings, and talked to them on comfortably non-technical subjects in the most ordinary language in the world. Workman has never read a line of Milton, as he frequently reminds one. He reads the *Dairy-Farmer's Gazette* every week, from cover to cover.

To each writer his own play and I am not suggesting that students should imitate Workman in every detail. The *Farmer's Weekly* is just as good to leave lying about as the *Gazette*. But basically, Workman was sound.

NEWSTATESMANSHIP AND DAMNED-GOOD-JOURNALIST PLAY

Writermen must live in constant awareness of the opposition between these two great gambits. There is a distinct flavour of good writing about the former, fatal to the latter. The morning paper critic has only to remember that he may not be able to write but he is a damned-good-journalist. Being a damned-good-journalist means that you must either praise the film (or book, or play) to the heights, or blame to the depths. Whether praise or blame is chosen depends, if you are a damned-good-journalist, on your last week's article. You must never praise or blame two weeks running.

In Newstatesmanship, on the other hand, definite pros and cons are barred: and they are difficult, anyway, because pro-ing and conning is never the best way of going one better.

'GO ONE BETTER OR YOU GO ONE WORSE'

In Newstatesmaning the critic must always be on top of, or better than, the person criticized. Sometimes the critic will be of feeble and mean intelligence. The subject of his criticism may be a man of genius. Yet he must get on top. How? the layman asks.

By the old process – of going one better. Hope-Tipping of Buttermere had never really read a book since his schooldays, much less formed an original judgement. But he specialized in his own variations on the formula. He would skim some review dealing with the author involved, find out the quality for which this author was most famous, and then blame him for not having enough of it.

H.-T. first made a name for himself in 1930 by saying that 'the one thing that was lacking, of course, from D. H. Lawrence's novels, was the consciousness of sexual relationship, the male and female element in life'.

Get the Hope-Tipping angle. Talk about the almost open sadism of Charles Lamb, or about Lytton Strachey as a master of baroque. 'The deep superficiality of Catullus' is Hope-Tipping's, too. Never, by any shadow of a chance, was there a hint of a cliché in the judgements of Hope-Tipping.

Another way of going one better is to be surprised. Thus: 'I am surprised that so eminent a scholar as Dr Whitefeet' ... 'We all owe a great debt to Dr Whitefeet'

... 'Where should we be without Dr Whitefeet?' Then go for him.

Learn how to smile good-humouredly at Dr Whitefeet's analysis of the early love poems of Sebastian Cromer. Say, 'surely it doesn't matter whether it was Paulette or Nina to whom Cromer was referring when he wrote "eyes twin pools of onyx". The important point for us who come after, surely, is that here is a man who lived, breathed, moved, and had his being. Nay, who loved with warm human passion, be she Paulette, Nina, or Proserpine herself.' This is the 'for God's sake' branch of the 'After all' section of writership.

Dr Whitefeet may be rather slow, but he will have a definite feeling that he is being got at, in some way.

Observe how, in Newstatesmanship, the critic is invariably a tremendous specialist in the subject under review, and must at all costs be more so than the author of the book discussed.

It doesn't matter if the subject is as remote as the study of Greek in Lower California, the reviewer must be there before. An easy method is to say, 'I am surprised that Mr Sprott does not give more credit, in the main body of his text, to that fine teacher and impeccable scholar Dr Kalamesa of Joinstown.' This is considered quite fair, even if you have never seen the name Kalamesa before, which, of course, you never will have, except in some footnote or appendix to Sprott's book.*

* J. Betjeman, in a series of conversations with me, has reminded me that in Reviewer's Basic, which he has studied for so many years, any attack on the author under review is essentially friendly. J. Betjeman has kindly turned aside from his second volume on *Periodship* to summarize for us his findings. They are as follows:

Friendly attacks should begin with faint praise, but be careful not to use adjectives or phrases of which the publisher can make

Remember, too, that it is utterly un-Newstatesmanlike to suggest that there is any branch of French literature with which you are not perfectly familiar. K. Digg was rightly banned from Newstatesmanship for stating in a middle page article that he had 'never read a word of Rimbaud'.

The absolute O.K.-ness of French literature, particularly modern French, and indeed of French generally, cannot be too much emphasized. K. Digg made a fool of himself, but everyone must respect the way Digg fought his way back for seven years, publishing in small provincial papers prefaces to catalogues of the exhibitions, in Dundee, of water-colours by children of operatives in jute manufacturing, etc. He would refer to France, somehow, every 250th word and end up with something boldly nostalgic. 'It is at this month of the year,' he would say,

use in advertisements. Safe faint praise adjectives are *catholic* – i.e. too wide in treatment to be anything but superficial; *well-produced* – i.e. badly written. Alternatively – 'The illustrations, of course, are excellent.' *Painstaking* – i.e. dull.

Useful words for friendly attacks are *awareness, interesting, tasteful, observant*.

Effective methods of attack are:

(i) To quote from a book no one else has read but you.

(ii) To imply that you are in some college or institution where the subject under review is daily discussed, so, of course, you know better but think this author quite good for one who has not had your opportunities of acquiring more knowledge.

(iii) To begin 'Serious students will perhaps be puzzled . . .'

(iv) To say 'In case there should be a Second Edition . . .' Then note as many trivial misprints as you can find.

It may well be that the author you are reviewing is someone who may be useful to you in the future. In that event write one signed and favourable review, and attack the book anonymously in another review in *The Times Literary Supplement* or the *Listener*. These papers specialize in unsigned friendly attacks and so do most antiquarian journals.

in his gramophone notes for the *Cumberland Farmer*,
'that one is dreaming once again of the brilliant colours
of the *Cotelons*, whisking and flirting their way between
the rotting stanchions of the bridge at Perpignan, while
the cool wind, the Dordogne wind, lifts miraculously
from the lake, and the garden, and its unkept shrub-
beries, still tangled with corpiscula, as it was when
Baudelaire's Remus swam in it.' The part about 'swam in
it' may sound weak, but everybody realized that Digg
was making a fight of it, and now, of course, all is for-
given and forgotten and Digg is back in Newstatesmanship we hope for good.

DAILY MIRRORSHIP

It should not be, but alas is, necessary to remind critics
that for Newstatesmanship it is essential to mix in with
the knowledge of French an unaffected love of tremendously ordinary and homely things like Danny Kaye,
mild and bitter, the *Daily Mirror*, the Bertram Mills
circus, and Rita Hayworth. This will show that, like all
really great authors, you write for, live among, and
primarily appeal to, the ordinary common people.

NOTES

Dedicationship. A. C. Y. Davis invented a means of word-
ing his dedications so that criticism of his book was practically
impossible, e.g. 'To PHYLLIS, in the hope that one day
God's glorious gift of sight may be restored to her.' Critics
and reviewers naturally felt it would be bad taste to be rude
about Davis's book (*Spring on the Arun*) with such a dedica-
tion. Only I knew that Phyllis was, in fact, Davis's great-
grandmother, extremely short-sighted, it is true. And not
surprisingly at the age of ninety-six.

I'm Afraidmanship. 'I'm afraid' is a splendid life phrase

and admirable for showing that you are a nice man and that
the reader is a nice man and that your book is a nice book.

I'm afraid I don't like politics . . . mysticism. . . .

RILKING

Just as there are O.K.-words in conversationship, so there
are O.K.-*people to mention* in Newstatesmanship. Easily
the most O.K. for 1945–50 are Rilke and Kafka.* It is
believed that they will still be absolutely O.K. for another five years, in fact it is doubtful if there have been
any more O.K.-names in recent times. This gambit is
called 'Rilking'.†

A NOTE ON RECOMMENDED LIMELIGHT PLAY

Lifemen must always remember that whatever the facts,
indeed, whatever the facts the more so, they must always
be one degree busier than anyone else.

Our model for this must, of course, be Gattling-Fenn,
Number One Limelight for ever in our hearts.

I noticed Gattling's methods the first time I met
him. One had the impression, even then, that he was a
pretty famous man, yet he called me by my Christian

---

* In 1937 Lorca was O.K., too.

† *Anti-Rilking.* There are types of authors who are not O.K.
names whom it is O.K. to pitch into. It is all right to pitch into:

Any author who has written a book about dogs.

Any author who has written a book on natural history, illus-
trated with woodcuts.

Any author who has written a life of Napoleon, Byron, or Dr
Johnson, without footnotes or bibliography.

Any author of a life of anybody not yet dead.

Any author of a book on Sussex.

Any author of a book of unrhymed and irregular verse in the
style of 1923.

Any author of a book of thoughtful open-air poems in the style
of 1916.

name at once. In fact I heard his voice saying, 'Hullo, Stephen', before I got into the room. He asked me how I was, and I said as a matter of fact I had just been in bed with a cold.

He said: 'How lucky you are to be able to go to bed with a cold.'

Another thing I noticed about Gattling, that wherever he was, whether he was sitting on the steps of the Members' Enclosure at Cheltenham, or pausing for a sandwich lunch half-way up the Cairngorms, he would always, at one point, pull out a roll of galley proofs and start correcting them.

Though obviously always extremely busy, he was obviously always most frightfully calm.*

* Needless to say, Gattling had been in films, and, in fact, there was a general impression that he had made a tremendous name for himself as a director, when, brilliantly, I am told, he was not calm at all, but feverish, enhancing this effect by crunching up a benzedrine tablet every five minutes. These tablets were, in fact, dummies, being made of sugar and water in solidified form.

Fig. 13 False benzedrine tablet, magnified 7½ times (Lifemanship Accessories). A genuine benzedrine tablet (below) is drawn to same scale for comparison.

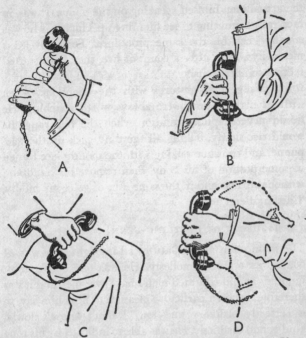

Fig. 14. MOUTHPIECE BLOCKING for Important Person Play. While caller is talking, take little notice but continue your conversation with friends in the room, covering mouthpiece 'with the natural ease of long custom' (Pettigrew). *Not* (*a*) by placing hand on mouthpiece but by placing mouthpiece either against elbow (*b*), thigh (rectus femoris) (*c*), or back of head (*d*).

This calmness of Gattling was emphasized by his habit of arriving two minutes early for an appointment, dictating answers to his letters as he read them through, and showing special knowledge of telephone management.

TELEPHONE MANAGEMENT

He would never, under any circumstances, speak to any man until his secretary had got not only his secretary but the actual man himself speaking on the phone. It was, in fact, rather amusing to see him ring up Tipping, who was equally keen on the same procedure. They devised a means by which, after a count of five, they both started talking simultaneously.

But his general gestures with the telephone, when without his secretary, were always worth watching. He would never express irritation when the bell rang; he would rise slowly, talking all the time, pick up the telephone, and continue talking with the mouthpiece buried in some portion of his body, then remove his hand and without a pause and in the same tone of voice say mildly, 'Gattling-Fenn here.'

THE MODESTY OF GATTLING-FENN

The main point about Gattling's Limelight Play was, of course, its essential modesty. He was one of the most ignorant and ill-educated men I have ever met, and it was therefore always a particular pleasure to hear him say, to a perfectly ordinary question, 'I don't know,' slowly, kindly, and distinctly. He was able to indicate, by his tone of voice, that although he knew practically everything about practically everything, and almost everything about this really, yet the mere fact that he knew such a tremendous lot about it made him realize, as we couldn't possibly, that the question was so inextricably two-sided that only a smart-Alec would ever dream of trying to pass judgement either way.

Another characteristic of Fenn was his absolutely unspeakable kindness to underlings, on those rare occasions when for five or six weeks he did manage to hold down some kind of directorship. He would enter into discussions with his inferiors exactly as if he was one of them. His favourite phrase was, 'I am going to stick my neck

Fig. 15. LIMELIGHT PLAY: HOW TO BE PHOTOGRAPHED IN
PUBLIC. A. *Right.* B. *Wrong.* Note: These sketches were drawn
from life by Colonel Wilson, who made a special tour of fashion-
able restaurants, etc. Genuine press photographers were present
and we note that the male figure in sketch A was in the habit of
paying £50 for the publication of these and similar photographs
of himself and partner.

out, but —' (to show, as it were, how unsycophantic he was to himself).

But Fenn certainly deserved the success he achieved by his really splendid management of public appearances, speeches after dinner, etc.

He knew exactly the expression to put on when being photographed. Having previously bribed the photographer to take his photograph, he would, of course, when the photographer approached him, demur. He would certainly not look pleased, but a little down and a little pained. If in a restaurant, he would see that there were no glasses on his table, except one obviously containing water. He would even bewilder neighbours at the next table by suddenly putting six of his used glasses and a bottle of brandy on their table.

If he was being photographed in a group, he would try and make out, by an encouraging glance, that it was somebody else who ought to be in the foreground, and he would lean forward to speak to the least important person present.

At a public dinner, he would be a tremendously good listener to the least important person near him, taking no notice whatever of the chairman. If Gattling's name was mentioned in a speech and there was applause, he would drag to his feet some confused stranger who had nothing to do with it.

'We all know to whom we owe the "Fenn Wing" as it has been called,' the chairman would say. And once it had been clearly established that the applause was directed at Fenn, who had fiddled the cement rights in the transaction, he pulled to his feet, I remember, a harmless Old Marlburian who happened, through confusing the Pinafore Room at the Savoy with the Princess Ida, to be attending the wrong dinner.

6

LIFEMANSHIP RESEARCH

*Lifemanship is in its early stages still: but our young
workers have not been idle.*

MUSIC

THE general aim in music is to make other people feel
outside it – or outsiders, compared to yourself. Don't look
too solemn when music is played; on the contrary, be
rather jolly about your musical appreciation. Say,
'Yes, it's a grand tune, isn't it?' and bawl it out in a
cracked, unmusical voice. Say, 'Ludwig suggests that
this theme represents the galloping hooves of the Four
Horsemen of the Apocalypse. But to me it's just a grand
tune.'

Suggestions for conductorship continue to pour in. W.
Goehr, coming north to preside over the Pennine Northern Orchestra, who for twelve years had taken their lead
from the first violin and paid no attention to the baton of
any visiting conductor, got the better of these men, many
of whom came from Bradford, by a piece of what I can
only call brilliant conductorship.

It was a new work by Mahler. The night before the
rehearsal, he altered a B flat to a B natural in a fortissimo
passage of the score of the 7th double bass. When the
passage was played in rehearsal, he stopped instantly.
'Someone is playing B natural instead of B flat,' he said.
In the long, brawling argument which ensued, Goehr, of
course, came out on top, and the Pennine Northern,
although they did not change their fixed expressions, did

express, or so it seemed to me at the time, some sort of silent approval.

Talking over a concert afterwards, with someone who has been there in another part of the hall, it is not a bad thing to say, in a tone of faint interest: 'What, you stayed for the Debussy?'

ACTORSHIP

R. Simpson (the originator of Simpson's Statue [see *Gamesmanship*, p. 65]) is, of course, also an actor. Not only that, he is the genial secretary and leading light of the Actorship Society, busy now collecting ploys and amusing gambits. His own 'Simpson Specials' as he calls them can be briefly described:

(1) If a young actor who shows signs of becoming a rival is slightly 'pressing' in rehearsal, tell him afterwards that 'he's never played the scene better'. The chances are that, next time, he will over-act badly, and even lose his touch with the part for good.

(2) The *V-shaped smile*, for fellow-actors who are doing rather well. Stand in the wings and be seen by them clapping soundlessly, as if to encourage.

(3) If an actor has, to your disappointment, been given a part larger than your own, and one which you secretly coveted, take an opportunity of saying to him, quietly and sympathetically, at the beginning of the *second* week of rehearsal: 'My God, you've got a pill!'

WORK IN PROGRESS (with names of directing Lifemen)

FIELD-GLASSES PROCEDURE. When to have field-glasses which are so big that they are actually too heavy to hold; and when to have them so small and inconspicuous that they do not, in fact, magnify at all. (A 'Friend of Lifemanship', Luton.)

ROYALTYSHIP. The playing of, or threat to play, still ball games, especially golf, in a crown. (A. King.*)

FOREIGN TRAVEL PLAY. (We'll Go Roamin' Branch.) Having booked up hotels all along your route three months in advance, say, 'We're just going to bung our car over the Channel and let it follow its own nose.' (G. Barry.)

CARSHIP. How to deliver over the map to your passenger to read, saying you'll 'leave the route to her', and then not leave the route to her but, on the contrary, question every turning so that in the end she confuses north with south, and third-class roads with the signs for windmills. (G. Tsu, Bulawayo.)

GENIUSSHIP. Our Bermondsey group is working on this large and complex ploy. This includes limpmanship, being the son of a tinker, importance of mother, unimportance of father, being different from other boys and wandering off alone in fields with a book, being like other boys only more so, leaving weaker work till later, showing kindliness, goodwill, and understanding of others, being absolutely impossible.

DANCINGSHIP. If everyone else is dancing violently, separating from their partners, twirling round on separate axes, etc., how to move slowly and statuesquely, and indicate reproof and superiority by such movement.

How, alternatively, if the dancing is fairly prim, to suggest that this good form is bad form, or at any rate faintly Park Crescent, by being the only pair in the room to dance bebop.

HOUSE WARMINGSHIP. How to comment on a friend's new house. How to say you like it ... that you think they've got round the awkwardnesses admirably ... that, of course, they had to have the window there you

* Pseudonym of well-known King.

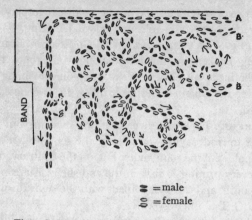

☰ = male
☷ = female

Fig. 16. DANCINGSHIP (see page 81). (i) Counter Bad Form Play. Note Lifeman's Path of Disassociation on the perimeter.

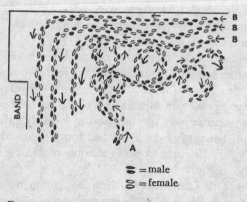

☰ = male
☷ = female

DANCINGSHIP. (ii) Counter Good Form Play. 'A' represents Lifeman's movements throughout.

supposed ... and would have to make another one there ... that it's from next door, of course, that you get the really wonderful view ... that it's much better to have the original coverings if you can't get new ones made ... that aren't they wise to leave the walls in their original colour – God knows you have to stand over them nowadays to get the colour you really want.

PERIODSHIP. How to specialize in periods which have not yet been specialized. Note on the Coca-Cola period. How to be writing a book on the revival of the Gothic Revival. Lifemanship's *Twopenny List of Unbooked Dates*, for period hunters.

UNDERGRADUATESHIP. Our older Universities are rightly conservative in their introduction of new subjects to their list of studies. There is, as yet, no School of Gameslifemanship. But at Oxford, if not Cambridge, a Research Fellowship is under discussion, and accredited Students already exist. Their researches, in process of coordination at Yeovil, rightly seem to concentrate on the essential Undergraduate Situation – the Student-Don syndrome, exemplified in its greatest purity in the weekly visit when Undergraduate reads to Tutor his essay on the theme set the week before.

P. Lewis, expert in Oxford Undergraduateship, has set it down as basic to this ploy that

where the Layman would concentrate on his subject, the Gamesman* *concentrates on his tutor.*

Clothesmanship can be used as a distraction in mid-tutorial.

That accomplished Old Hand, G. Cartwright, reduced a shy, shabby Arts don to near-speechlessness for a term by

* For 'Gamesman' now (September) read 'Lifeman' throughout.

consistently turning up in breeches, boots, and spurs, and disappearing at intervals during the interview with the remark, 'Mind if I slip out and see if my horse is all right? You know how restless they get after a hard day.'

There may be good pre-game work to be done the day before. Thus:

GAMESMAN: Oh, excuse me. I just wanted to check a point with you. Was this week's subject, 'The League Machinery AND the Settlement of Disputes' or 'The League Machinery IN the Settlement of Disputes'?
DON: I'm not quite sure. I think it was 'and', but ...
GAMESMAN: Ah yes. 'And'. Good. Fortunately all my reading has been on that supposition.

It used to be said of that illustrious pioneer, E. von Th., that he had so perfected the tone of annihilating contempt with which he used to read out the titles he had been given to write about (he was reading History) that he was ultimately asked to *choose the subjects himself*.

A. Thornton writes brilliantly* of Donmanship, suggesting Counters.
Donmanship he defines as the 'art of Criticizing without Actually Listening'.

The experienced Donsman has a store of telling matchpoints. He challenges all comers by letting it be known that he has a Special Subject, the emphasis falling on the adjective. It may be Turkish Personnel at the Battle of Lepanto, or, Some Unformulated Ideas current in the Eighteenth Century. Timid Donsmen sometimes overstep the mark and confine themselves too rigidly to marginal topics, e.g. Assyrian Woodwind Instruments. But it is a sign of the skilled and formidable Donsman to pick a topic on which there are not only

* The full text of all these passages is to be found in the Research Sections of February 1950 numbers of the *Isis*.

No Books, but No Formed View At All (e.g. the Fourth French Republic), thus scoring an immense lead, or reputation.

In one of his passages A. Thornton ends on a note of what I can only call nostalgic rhetoric which moved me as I hope it will move you. I propose to quote it in full. And let me say now that when the lead passes into younger hands, I shall be the first to step back.

If the Gamesman feels at a disadvantage, playing as he does all matches away, he can inveigle Donsman on to his home ground, and employ Hostmanship on him. He may ask Donsman's opinion on a South African sherry. He may surround him with young Gamesmen and Gamesgirls all talking about 'The Third Man', which either Donsman has not seen, or, if he has, thought it merely a thriller. If young, he can leave feeling old; if old, doubtful. Gamesgirls are a convenience here. Rules of play are of course more sharply defined in this more enclosed space than elsewhere, but a well-matched pair will welcome the more exacting demands of the Great Game.

There are, indeed, no limits to the ramifications and interpretations of this constant struggle. Let Donsmen always delight to baffle Gamesmen, Gamesmen ever seek new means of outwitting Donsmen. Character is tempered, and the world gains.

K.C.MANSHIP (A. Hawke's gambit)

A. Hawke's work on *K.C.manship* is still unpublished but he has allowed me to include here this example of his work.

Hawke's gambit may be summarized as follows:

If he, Hawke, is opposed by Y, K.C. (someone else), and if, during the final stages of the case, Y, K.C., speaking of some prosecution ploy of Hawke's says 'My learned

friend has made a point which is of the utmost importance. It is indeed an issue which stands at the root of the
British penal system. Legal history is being made in this
court today. But . . .', then at the word 'but', Hawke gets
up, and walks, unobtrusively and indifferently, out of the
building.

7

GAMESMANSHIP RESEARCH

It is our purpose here to summarize some of the recent findings of the Gamesmanship Research Committee. Thousands of people, or certainly scores, have sent in their recommendations for new gamesploys and gambits. Our task is to sift, and to coordinate.

A SUMMARY OF RECENT WORK ON
GOLFMANSHIP

ALWAYS remember that it is in golf that the skilful gamesman can bring his powers to bear most effectively. The constant companionship of golf, the cheery contact, means that *you are practically on top* of your opponent, at his elbow. The novice, therefore, will be particularly susceptible to your gambits.

Remember the basic rules. Remember the possibilities of defeat by tension. Recorded elsewhere is the 'Flurry', as it is called, in relation to lawn tennis. *It is an essential part of Winning Golf.* The atmosphere, of course, is worked up long before the game begins. Here is the golf variant of Flurry.

Your opponent is providing the car. You are a little late. You have forgotten something. Started at last, suggest that, 'Actually we ought to get rather a move on – otherwise we may miss our place.'

'What place?' says the opponent.

'Oh, well, it's not a bad thing to be on the first tee on

time.' Though no time has been fixed, Opponent will soon be driving a little fast, a little tensely, and after you have provided one minor misdirection, he arrives at the clubhouse taut.

In the locker room one may call directions to an invisible steward or non-existent timekeeper. 'We ought to be off at 10.38.' 'Keep it going for us,' and so forth.

OPPONENT: Who's that you're shouting to?
GAMESMAN: Oh, it's only the Committee man for starting times.

Your opponent will be rattled, and be mystified, too, if he comes out to find the course practically empty.

If for some reason it happens to be full, you can put into practice Crowded Coursemanship, and suggest, before every other shot Opponent plays, that 'We mustn't take too long – otherwise we shall have to signal that lunatic Masterman, behind us, to come through. Then we're sunk.'

Here are some notes on certain general gamesmanship plays, in their relation to golf.

MIXED FOURSOMES

In a mixed foursome it is important in the basic foursome play (i.e. winning the admiration of your opponent's female partner) that your own drive should be longer than that of the opposing man, who will, of course, be playing off the same tee as yourself.

Should he possess definite superiority in length, you must either (a) be 'dead off my drive, for some reason' all day – a difficult position to maintain throughout eighteen holes; (b) say 'I'm going to stick to my spoon off the tee,' and drive with a Fortescue's Special Number 3 – an ordinary driver disguised to look like a spoon, and named 'spoon' in large letters on the surface of the head; (c) use the Frith-Morteroy counter.

The general play in mixed foursomes, however, differs widely from the Primary Gambits of a men's four. But beginners often feel the lack of a cut-and-dried guide.

In the all-male game, of course, when A and B are playing against C and D, the usual thing, if all is going well, is for A and B to be on delightfully good terms with each other, a model of easy friendship and understanding. Split Play is only brought into play by the A-B partnership if C-D look like becoming two up. A then makes great friends with C, and is quietly sympathetic when D, C's partner, makes the suspicion of an error, until C is not very unwillingly brought to believe that he is carrying the whole burden. His dislike for D begins to show plainly. D should soon begin to play really badly.

In the mixed game, all is different. *Woo the opposing girl* is the rule. To an experienced mixed-man like Du Carte, the match is a microcosm of the whole panorama of lovers' advances.

He will start by a series of tiny services, microscopic considerations. The wooden tee picked up, her club admired, the 'Is that chatter bothering you?' The whole thing done with suggestions, just discernible, that her own partner is a little insensitive to these courtlinesses, and that if only he were her partner, what a match they'd make of it.

Du Carte, meanwhile, would be annoying the opposing man, by saying that 'Golf is only an excuse for getting out into the country. The average male is shy of talking about his love for birds and flowers. But isn't that ... after all –'

Du Carte was so loathsome to his male friends at such

moments that they became over-anxious to win the match. Whereas the female opponent, on the contrary, was beginning to feel that golf was not perhaps so important as sympathetic understanding.

By the twelfth hole Du Carte was able to suggest, across the distance of the putting green, that he was fast falling in love. And by the crucial sixteenth, Female Opponent would have been made to feel not only that Du Carte had offered a proposal of marriage, but that she, shyly and regretfully, had refused him.

Du Carte invariably won these matches two and one. For he knew the First Law of Mixed Gamesmanship: that *No woman can refuse a man's offer of marriage and beat him in match play at the same time.*

ADVANCED CADDIE PLAY

Remember the basic rule: *Make friends with your caddie and the game will make friends with you.* How true this is. It is easy to arrange that your guest opponent shall be deceived into under-tipping his caddie at the end of the morning round, so that the news gets round, among the club employees, that he is a no good, and the boys will gang up against him.

I, myself, have made a special study of Caddie Play, and would like to put forward this small suggestion for a technique of booking a caddie for your guest.

There is usually one club caddie who is an obvious half-wit, with mentally deficient stare and a complete ignorance of golf clubs and golf play. *Do not choose this caddie for your opponent. Take him for yourself.* There is such a caddie in my own Club. He is known as Mouldy Phillips. It is obvious from a hundred yards that this poor fellow is a congenital. While preparing for the first tee say:

SELF: I'm afraid my caddie isn't much to look at.

OPPONENT: Oh, well.

SELF: He's a bit – you know.

OPPONENT: Is he?

SELF: I was anxious you shouldn't get him.

OPPONENT: But –

SELF: It's all right, I know the course. (*Then, later, in a grave tone.*) It gives him such a joy to be asked.

OPPONENT: Why?

SELF: Oh – I don't think they'd ever have taken him on here if I hadn't been a bit tactful about it.

It is possible to suggest that in the case of Mouldy you have saved a soul from destitution. Impossible in such circumstances for your friend to refer to, much less complain of, Mouldy's tremor of the right arm, which swings like the pendulum of a grandfather clock, to the hiccoughs or the queer throat noise he will make in the presence of strangers – habits to which you are accustomed.

Meanwhile you have succeeded in your promise to get for Opponent the best caddie on the course. A man like Formby. 'He's just back from caddieing in the Northern Professional,' you say. So he is, and your friend soon knows it. During the first hole:

SELF: I suppose Formby knows this course better than anyone in the world.

FORMBY: Ought to, sir.

Your opponent will feel bound, now, to ask advice on every shot, every club. Formby is certain to give it to him, in any case. After he has done a decent drive and a clean iron shot, Formby will probably say: 'Playing here last week, Stranahan reached this point, with his brassie, *from the tee.* Yes, he can hit, that man.' Here one hopes that Mouldy Phillips will say something.

MOULDY: AA–ooo–rer–oh.
SELF: Jolly good, Mouldy. Yes, he's got us there, old boy.

Here Opponent should be not only distracted but mystified. Formby will redouble his advice, while in contrast Mouldy looks on with delighted admiration at everything I do.

LEFT-HAND-RIGHT-HAND-PLAY

I believe it was O. Sitwell who devised this simple rule for play against left-handers. If (as so often happens) your opponent, though left-handed in games generally, yet plays golf with ordinary right-hand clubs, it is a good thing, during the first hole *after the fifth* which he plays badly, to say:

SELF: Do you mind if I say something?
L.H.: No. What?
SELF: Have you ever had the feeling that you are *playing against the grain?*
L.H.: No – how do you mean?
SELF: Well, you're really left-handed, aren't you?
L.H.: I certainly am – except for golf.
SELF: Have you ever been tempted to make the big change?
L.H.: How do you mean?
SELF: Play golf left-handed as well. Chuck those clubs away. Fling them into the bonfire. Damn the expense – and get a brand-new set of left-handed clubs.
L.H. Yes, but –
SELF: *You know* that is your natural game. Be extravagant.

L.H.: It isn't the expense –
SELF: Money doesn't mean anything nowadays, anyhow.
L.H.: I mean –
SELF: Everybody's income's the same, really.

The fact that your opponent has been advised to play right-handedly by the best professional in the country will make him specially anxious to prove by his play that you are in the wrong. The usual results follow. If he is not only a left-hander but plays with left-handed clubs as well, the same conversation will do, substituting the word *right* for *left* where necessary.

BEMERONDSAY TROPHY PLAY

C. Bemerondsay was an awkward, tricksy, inventive gamesman, full of devices, many of them too complicated for the older generation. I remember he tried to upset me once by 'letting it be known,' that his name 'of course' was pronounced 'Boundsy', or some such nonsense. Players uncertain of their position were, it is believed, actually made to feel awkward by this small gambit, and I have heard G. Carter – always conscious that his own name was a wretchedly unsuitable one for a games player – apologize profusely for his 'stupid mispronunciation'.

On the other hand, Bemerondsay's Cup Trick is well worth following. I will briefly summarize it.

In play against a man like Julius Wickens, who goes in for suggesting he was once much better than he is, the dialogue runs as follows:

BEMERONDSAY: I have a feeling you know more about the game than you let on.
WICKENS: Oh, I don't know.
BEMERONDSAY: What *is* your golf history?

WICKENS: Well, just before the war I was winning
things a bit.

BEMERONDSAY: I bet you were.

WICKENS: Spoons – and things.

BEMERONDSAY: Oh, you did, did you?

WICKENS: Then in 1931 I won a half share in the July
tea-tray – rather nice.

BEMERONDSAY: Very nice, indeed.

After the match, Bemerondsay asked Wickens round
for a drink after the game. 'I keep the stuff in my snug-
gery,' he says, and in they go.

'Somebody must have put the drink in the cupboard,'
says Bemerondsay. 'Why?'

He opens the cupboard door and to his 'amazed surprise' out falls a small avalanche of golf cups, trophies,
silver golf balls, engraved pewter mugs, symbolical groups
in electroplate. 'Oh, hell,' says Bemerondsay slowly.

WICKENS (*really impressed*): These all yours?

BEMERONDSAY: Yes. This is my tin.

WICKENS: When did you win all these?

BEMERONDSAY: I never know where to put it.

It is of no importance in the gambit, but it is believed
by most gamesmen that these 'trophies' of Bemerondsay
really are made of tin or silver-painted wood, or that at
any rate they were bought by Bemerondsay as a job lot.
It is doubtful whether he had ever entered for a Club
competition, as he was a shocking match player.

FAILURE OF TILE'S INTIMIDATION PLAY

Americans visiting this country for a championship have
sometimes created a tremendous effect by letting it be
known that, on the voyage over, in order to keep in

practice, they drove new golf balls from the deck of the *Queen Mary* into the Atlantic.

I believe that W. Hagen brilliantly extended this gambit by driving balls from the roof of the Savoy Hotel.

When they came to our own seaside course, to play in the Beaverbrook International Tournament, two Americans created a tremendous effect by driving new balls into the sea before the start, to limber up.

E. Tile, pleased with this, determined to create a similar impression before his match against Miss Bertha Watson, in our June handicap. He cleverly got hold of six old or nearly worthless balls, value not more than twopence each, painted them white, and teed them up twenty yards from the cliff edge to drive them into Winspit Bay. By bad luck, however, not one of his shots reached the edge of the cliff, much less the sea. So his stratagem was discovered.

G. ODOREIDA

G. Odoreida, I am glad to say, did not often play golf. By his sheer ruthlessness, of course, Odoreida could shock the most hardened gamesman. Woe to the man who asked him as a guest to his golf club.

He would start with some appalling and unexpected thrust. He would arrive perhaps in a motor-propelled invalid chair. Why? Or his hair would be cropped so close to the head that he seemed almost bald.

Worse still, he would approach some average player of dignified and gentlemanly aspect and, for no reason, *ask for his autograph*. Again, why? One was on tenterhooks, always.

I remember one occasion on which his behaviour was suspiciously orthodox. The club was Sunningdale. 'Thank heaven,' I thought, 'such ancient dignity pervades these precincts that even Odoreida is subdued'.

I introduced him to the secretary. It was a bold move, but it seemed to work. I was anxious when I saw, however, that on that particular afternoon the secretary was inspecting the course. As he came near us Odoreida was near the hole. Without any reason, he took an iron club from his bag and took a wild practice swing in the very edge, if not the actual surface, of the green. A huge piece of turf shot up. 'Odoreida!' I said, and put the turf back with an anxious care that was perfectly genuine.

Two holes later the secretary was edging near us again. Odoreida was about to putt. He took the peg from the hole and *plunged it into the green.* 'Odoreida!' I cried

Fig. 17. ONLY KNOWN PORTRAIT OF ODOREIDA (A), with ordinary Pyrenean short-haired mastiff drawn to same scale (B).

once more. Surely, this time, the secretary must have seen. But I remember very little of the rest of the afternoon's play. I know that Odoreida won by 7 and 5. I am glad to say that I refused to play the remaining holes.

In other words, gamesmanship can go too far. And the gamesman must never forget that his watchwords, frequently repeated to his friends, must be sportsmanship and consideration for others.

R. AND A.-MANSHIP

I am delighted that the R. and A., after the usual delays of conservatism and the Old Guard at St Andrews, have come into line with the spirit, if not with the individual rulings, of the findings of the Gamesmanship Council, 681 Station Road, Yeovil.

It is now the function of Station Road, we conceive, to interpret the new rules in the gamesmanlike spirit of their conception, adding a tip here, a suggestion there.

What a good idea it is, for instance, to place greater emphasis on Etiquette, if possible, than Rules. If Opponent retries his putt he has not broken a rule, and you may feel disposed to point this out to him. But it is against the etiquette of golf. This you will not point out to him, but your expression will become fixed, and distant, for a suitable period.

This will put off many novice gamesmen, but beware of the counter from the old hand. Odoreida, in play against Wickham, after deliberately re-trying short putts, all of which he had missed, on the first four greens, 'suddenly noticed' Wickham's fixed expression on the fifth tee.

ODOREIDA: You look a bit cheap. What's the matter? Hangover or something?'
WICKHAM: Really!

Wickham's retort was weak, inevitably, and equally inevitably he lost the match.

New Rules, as a fact in themselves, are an aid to gamesmen. Your opponent will never be quite clear which rules have been altered, and an atmosphere of doubt can be lightly intensified. If putts are equidistant from the hole you can say, 'Who putts first? I believe, now, it must be decided by lot.' This rule has been unchanged, of course, for 250 years. Gamesmen can then add, 'But have we got any lots? You see?' Opponent will get fidgety.

DEEMCRAFT

Of classic gamesworthiness is the ruling that the 'player is the sole judge as to whether his ball is playable or unplayable.' Deemcraft Basic should follow this line. During some early hole which the gamesman by bad play has almost certainly lost already, let him deem *playable* a ball which is, say, half-way down a rabbit hole covered with brushwood. After four attempts to hack it out he picks up, but a good impression has been made, and not only will his opponent be scrupulously fair in his own interpretation but fail to see anything wrong till you have taken back your ball from a perfectly open lie in the heather in front of the tee at three holes in the second half of the match.

TROLLEYSHIP

No open reference is made in the new rules to the trolley caddie – that 'great new factor in golf gamesmanship', as Lord Morden has called it. But covert references to 'movable objects' are everywhere in the Rules, and it is obvious that trolleys have R. and A. approval.

We have developed trolleys for gamesmen on lines now familiar. Our 'KARRICLUB DUNSTABLE' has the squeak-

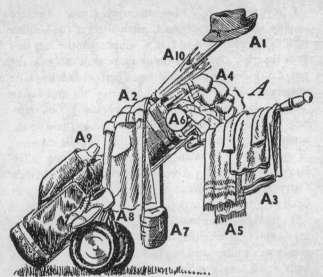

Fig. 18. COUNTER TROLLEY PLAY. Optimal normal loading of mean maximum impedimenta. KEY: *A*, Owner's original load (7 clubs). A, Opponent's load, numbered in order of fixment: A1, hat. A2, raincoat. A3, pullover. A4, spare wooden clubs. A5, towel. A6, spare irons. A7 birdwatching binoculars. A8, light shoes. A9, thermos containing lukewarm tea. A10, ordinary umbrella.

ing wheel, our 'HAUNTED HEATH' two holes drilled in the ironwork, which, if there is the faintest breeze, make, according to its inventor, J. L. Hodson, sounds beautifully suggestive of a mouth organ.

Counter trolley play is divided into two parts. Part One is for the gamesman who, in play against opponent with trolley, always has his clubs carried by the best available caddie in the club. His concern is for the physical well-being of his opponent. 'Easy up the slope with that thing,' he will say. 'Let me give you a hand.' Or 'Don't your fingers get frightfully hot/cold/wet/sticky?' (according to the weather).

I, however, strongly advocate carrying your own clubs in play against a trolleyman, particularly if the weather is hot. The ploy then is, first, to emphasize the fact that your superior youth and vitality make such things as the use of a trolley absurdly fiddling. Then act as follows. At near or about the seventh hole, *take off tie*, and saying 'May I hang it on your trolley thing?' insert it on opponent's trolley. Two holes later remove sweater and do the same thing. At the 12th, put all spare golf balls in pocket of opponent's bag, saying, 'This won't make any difference to you, will it?' Develop on these lines till 18th. Carry 'by accident' an old copy of an ABC or other heavy book in order to add to opponent's load.

T. Rattigan, who has long specialized in this gambit, uses a specially weighted tie, to add to the burden on his opponent's trolley; and has had made for him spare golf balls which look genuine enough, but which are in fact made of lead throughout.*

---

* These notes on Trolley Play originally appeared in the *Sunday Times*. They produced a strange 'reply' from T. Rattigan himself, calling my accuracy in question (*Sunday Times*, 25.vi.50). Both this 'reply' and my answer I reprint below, leaving the reader to form his own judgement.

To the Editor of the *Sunday Times*
SIR – Mr S. Potter, in his recent article on R. and A.-manship, most flatteringly made reference to my foolish trifling device of the weighted tie, for use in encumbering ones golf opponent's trolley caddy ('The Troll King, Mk III'), but incorrectly, I fear, ascribed to myself the invention of the lead golf balls (or 'Trolley-boggers') for which the credit must surely go to Mrs Bassett. That great gameswoman is, of course, already responsible for the hooting clubhead, adopted by the Gamesmanship Council as long ago as 1936, and for a more recent brilliancy, the reversible umbrella (obverse blue and yellow, reverse violet and rust) not yet submitted for official sanction, but the prototype of which she has already

used with remarkable effect in wet after-luncheon play at her home course, Tossem Down.

Having thus corrected our august President on a minor matter, may I now have the great temerity to suggest that he is also at fault on a major one – to wit, the whole question of New Rulesmanship? The heavy burden of his arduous administrative duties has, I fear, blinded the President to the fact that the various ploys which he advocates, and which formed the subject of a Council circular letter last January, have, in the rough hurly-burly of practical gamesmanship, long since been superseded by one all-embracing but very simple gambit. It is as follows.

At a given moment, preferably when the opponent has chipped to within a few feet of the pin, give a start of surprise, pull out from the hip pocket a copy of the new rules and, quickly flipping over the pages, study a passage at random with a grave and concentrated frown; after ten seconds raise the eyebrows; after a further ten, shake the head slowly from side to side; then replace book in hip pocket with, if necessary, a short, sharp laugh; finally, gaze thoughtfully at the horizon with the eyebrows in the elevated position, while the opponent addresses himself to his putt – or more correctly, to his putts.

T. RATTIGAN

Sunningdale

To the Editor of the *Sunday Times*

Sir – Mr Rattigan must have been joking when he suggested that 'Mrs Bassett' of 'Tossem [*sic*] Down invented the use of lead golf balls for adding weight to opponent's trolley caddy'. Winifred Bassett of Tosem was certainly the first gameswoman to use them, as long ago as 1946, just as, three years later, Mr Rattigan adopted this 'new' device for Sunningdale, a course beautifully adapted by nature for counter-trolley play. But the use of lead, or some alloy of this substance, is as old as gamesmanship itself, dating as it does from the covert substitution of a pure leaden ball when handing a 'wood' to your opponent for some vital shot at bowls.

Mr Rattigan suggests that I am 'too busy with administrative duties' to have heard of a certain New Rulesmanship ploy which consists in taking out a book of the new rules after opponent has chipped to the green, scanning a passage at random, shrugging the shoulders, shaking the head, etc., as opponent is about to putt. Let me say at once that so far from being ignorant of this not ineffective gambit, we have discarded it (B32688 Aug. 1950). The counter, of which Mr Rattigan seems to be unaware, consists in opponent snatching out *his* copy of the rules, showing an equally random passage to his caddy, and nodding in silent unison with the caddy till the gambiter has sheepishly had to put his own copy of the rules back in his pocket. This whole tedious evolution was, of course, the chief if not the only cause of the insufferable delays in the recent Amateur at St Andrews: and our Council is pleased to fall in with the wishes of the R. & A. by banning it.

Mr Rattigan is a keen young gamesman of distinct promise, Number Sixteen out of the forty seeded men in the forthcoming Gamesmanship Open. It would be a thousand pities if other entrants followed his example and engaged in long controversial arguments in the public press on the eve of the Championship. Good luck, Mr Rattigan; but let us leave 'the administrative work', and the codifications as well, to older and perhaps wiser heads.

S. POTTER

8

NOTE ON CHRISTMAS
GAMESMANSHIP

IT so happens that very little has been written about the art of winning Christmas games; yet there is no side of sport in which sloppy technique is more dismally common.

Yet what a field is Christmas for the gamesman. The reader will understand that there is only room here for a note on the basic principles.

The general atmosphere of Christmas family gatherings, with all their vague jolliness, noise, and sketchy goodwill, is a perfect *climate of operation* for the man who keeps his head. If during any game there is a doubt about the score (to give the classical example of Christmas Basic) it is perfectly safe for the man who knows as a fact that the score is one or two points against him, to try a 'let's call it all square', spoken in the friendly, what-does-it-matter-anyhow tone suitable to the friendly Christmas gathering.

Remember, first, that the essence of Christmas games is their local quality, with local rules, e.g. the rolling of pennies down a groove in the banisters. Sloppy gamesmanship is sometimes seen when one who wished to be regarded as a noted boxer or rugger player suggests that such games are not serious. The correct technique is to *know more about them than anybody else.* And, moreover, to suggest new versions and local variations on the family games, *which can be practised privately for a fortnight before the Christmas holiday*. Instead of the usual Blow Pong Ball (blowing a ping-pong ball into a goal across a table) it is 'much more fun' to use a hazel nut. With his previous practice in the special kind of spitting puff required, he will win easily.

The winning of such games may seem trivial, but it is of great help in the establishment, so essential, of what we call Christmas Control. *You* must be the jolly uncle who 'makes everything go'. It is *your* voice, first heard roaring with laughter in the hall, which cheers everybody up, and makes somebody say 'Hooray for Arthur!' or whatever the name may be. This ploy, known as Life and Soulmanship, is not always easy, and it may be necessary to get some fellow gamesman to shout, 'Come on, Arthur, you organize it.' It is even possible, sometimes, to shout 'Hooray for Uncle Arthur!' yourself, in a disguised voice, from behind a screen.

If a straightforward game – e.g. ordinary ping-pong – is suggested, you can then know a 'frightfully good home-made kind' which is played on a small *circular* table, with a net made of volumes, balanced back upwards, of the Home University Library. I have proved that *one day's* previous practice makes success certain.

Life and Soulmanship is even more essential in the great question of Child Play. Children are the special problem of Christmas games. It is, of course, their season – as it should be, I am glad to say – and the gamesman can at once make use of this fact. For if he wants to suggest a particularly complex card game which he alone can understand, he can whisper to some Mother:

'Do you know who will adore this? Little John.'

Christmas is always the season when we want children, above all, to have a good time. But it is also true that children in certain games needing quick movement have a tremendous advantage over us. It is rightly held, in Gamesmanship circles, that they should be handicapped, and the way to do it is this. In a game like Racing Demon (Pounce Patience or Prawn-eye), children of ten often win because their small hands are defter. Little asides can be given, starting with 'steady on'. Work on the suggestion that they are being too rough. 'No, don't do that, old man.' Then work up a 'fear' that the cards will be bent, and continue, perhaps, with 'mind the table'. I have even seen a meaningless but peremptory 'mind the carpet' work as well as anything.*

* *Remember Mrs Wilson*. Failing this, there is always what we call 'Remember Mrs Wilson'. Mrs Wilson is some guest to whom *just because* it is Christmas, we have (you indicate) to be especially considerate. Remember to be polite to Mrs Wilson. Remember not to shout in Mrs Wilson's ear. And remind the child who is at the crest of a winning streak, remind even the child who though winning is sitting quiet and comparatively silent that she 'mustn't be rough in front of Mrs Wilson'. And remember, if all else fails it is always possible to *remove* a child from a game saying 'It's time you had your little rest now.'

G. Odoreida did extremely well with older children and the mid-teens by telling them that the contest he was planning for them was a 'jolly game for Young People'. This had the effect of taking away from them any desire to win.

9

GAMESMANSHIP AND WOMEN

THE whole question of Women and Gamesmanship thrusts into the very roots of the science. There is scarcely a gambit which cannot be used, provided the *basic adaptation* is made, by women against men, and vice-versa.

Let us begin these brief notes with an example of one such gambit. For some readers the names 'Charles and Christabel' may strike a chord. These two remarkably tall, handsome lawn-tennis players frankly disliked each other in private life (there was some affair between them which went wrong). But for years they worked together most effectively as co-gamesters.

Procedure: Charles begins his singles match at the local club. A man's stiff singles. To start with, he plays purposely below his form. Then, with the score 4-1 against him, say, in the first set, by a pre-arranged signal Christabel would appear, to watch.* Her appearance blindingly smart, she makes a big entry, in the character of 'Charles's girl, come to back him up', Charles would immediately begin to drive and serve with more Zonk – would really get going, and if he could manage to win an ace service, Christabel would give him a smile of dazzling encouragement.

Charles's opponent turns gloomy. 'Oh God,' he thinks. 'He's going to play up to this girl.' Christabel, of course, takes not the slightest notice of this opponent.†

The effect of this attack is redoubled, of course, if

* In golf, this play is everywhere known as the 'Striking Stranger Gambit'. The girl should first appear on the tenth fairway.

† For Christabel's matches against women Charles would turn up late, in the same way: intent and ardent.

Charles's opponent has as his spectator some plain and dowdy niece or aunt, who looks stuffily indifferent to what is going on. O. Bousefield, however, had a brilliant counter to this. Bousefield's spectator-friend, Miss Grace Perry, was a girl of stupefying plainness: but when Charles's Christabel came on the scene, with smiles of ravished and ravishing admiration, Bousefield pretended suddenly to feel himself under no obligation to conceal his own idiotic 'devotion' to the frightful-looking girl, Miss Perry. He sent her a thousand glances, even blew her a few surreptitious kisses, and played *at* her all the time. Poor Charles, as we all remember, completely lost his game in a daze of bewildered and futile curiosity.

For women, it is now accepted that knowledge of Clothesmanship is all-important: and a good deal of useful putting-off can be achieved by a clever use of better clothes.*

Finally, what is the essential strategy of sex war in

* But beware of counters if Miss P. turns up in elegant and correct if dashing shorts. A celebrated woman violinist was able to cast a decided shadow over this visitor and her team by slipping on a skirt and saying, 'I'm sorry about this skirt – but we're under the shadow of our dear old president here, you know – the Countess of Hale. And she says the most awesome things if she sees a girl playing in shorts.'

Mrs Wilder, the golfer, three times a runner-up of York women, would prettily counter-clothe her opponent thus. It was, as it so often is, a question of inflexion. Mrs Wilder herself would spend well over an hour preparing face and costume if anything like a 'gallery' was to be expected for her match. Yet she had a superb way, on the first tee, of saying to her (probably much more humbly dressed) opponent: '*What* an attractive little skirt.' She was able to suggest, by her intonation, that the wearing of such a skirt constituted an obvious and painstaking challenge to the male element among the spectators, an effort to intrigue the course stewards, if not to influence the judgement of the umpire.

games? For the man who finds himself playing against a woman, in singles or mixed, a good working knowledge of the Chivalry Gambit is essential.

In lawn-tennis singles, he will begin perhaps by saying, 'The male is allowed this one prerogative, I hope. Do please take choice of side and service.' If this does not have the desired effect of flustering the girl into making the man a present of the first game as she attempts to serve against the sun, it will yet start the average woman off on the wrong foot.

At golf, little attentions, such as picking up the woman's golf-bag for her, will have the same effect, especially if on the one occcasion when the woman really wants help with her clubs (scrambling up a steep hill) this little attention is forgotten.

In lawn-tennis mixed, the basic chivalry move is to pretend to serve less fiercely to the woman than the man. This is particularly useful if your first service tends to be out in any case.*

And what is the woman's counter to the chivalry gambit? Remember, in general don't react *against* the chivalry move. Appear to be hoodwinked by it – and if your male opponent shows the least signs of trying the 'I have long adored you from afar' move, treat it immediately as a formal proposal of marriage which you *shyly accept*. This is one of the most devastating, the most match-winning, counters in the whole realm of gamesmanship.

---

* There is, to me, an element of hatefulness about Odoreida's gambit in Counter Woman Play. He carried about with him a two-page privately-printed pamphlet called, I believe, *Why Women Cannot Play Squash Rackets*. On page 3 of this there was a large diagram of the female skeleton with the thigh-bones coloured ultramarine.

10

HOME AND AWAYMANSHIP

LOCAL gamesmen continue to do fine work for the Technique, and in the provinces they can often be seen in groups comparing the results of their small researches, notebook in hand, dipping into the local, perhaps, for a 'quick one', and sending results to our Yeovil headquarters, where there is an unpaid organization which places their findings in some file.

From these tiny beginnings – the chance finding of a Local Report in a waste-paper basket, perhaps – has sprung a flourishing band of enthusiasts for Playing Fields Play, or, as it is now more usually called, Home and Awaymanship.

There is certainly far too much genuine good spirit displayed in the treatment of visiting teams; and it is my object in this chapter to suggest some easy correctives.

Do not make your side of the preliminary exchange of notes fixing the date of the match too friendly. On the contrary, start the letter 'Dear Sir' and after signing it, type 'P.P. Signed in absence' at the end. Say: 'We usually make up our fixture list eighteen months in advance, but we do happen to have one date in the month you suggest.'

This long-range work eventually produces a certain nervousness or stiffness in your opponents without actually increasing their pugnacity.

Against teams visiting you for the first time a friendlier tone can be used to create what we call a 'ploy situation'. Say: 'You might care to catch an earlier train than the 10.15 if it would amuse you to "do" our little town and see round it for yourselves in the morning.' This will tire the team not only by making them take a much earlier train than necessary (a good ploy in any case), but also they will be wearied of dispirited tramping, particularly if there are no sights more worth seeing than an exhibition of shawls in the annexe to the Town Hall, and a statue of William IV in the public recreation ground.

A still matier tone can be used in this way.

'We shan't turn out to meet you with the red carpet,' you say, 'because in fact the Playing Fields are dead opposite the Station. Turn right and the entrance is diagonally opposite, by the next street.'

The meaninglessness of this direction is not realized till the team find after twenty minutes' search (carrying heavy sports bags) that the playing field they have at last found is the wrong one.

Of course, experienced teams will know how to counter this sort of thing by taking no notice whatever of any directions sent by post, and by coming with a small compass, or, even better, large-scale map.

There are, of course, many counters to these effective gambits and often the real battle is fought in the sports pavilion and changing-room, and we get all the pretty by-play of Homeship *versus* Awaymanship.

The offering of extremely feeble lunches to the visitors, for instance, can be countered, if the visiting team is forewarned, by the sudden and unexpected production by them of luncheon hampers, *no part of which, however much is left over, they offer to their hosts.*

The great master of Awaymanship was J. Scott-Dickens. A poor footballer, he was yet for twenty-three years chosen as captain when his side was playing away. He built up his attack by a multiplication of very small ploys. He would make a point, for instance, of mistaking the 12th man for the captain of the opposing side and

Fig. 19. Corner of Visitors' Changing-room at Basing-stoke. (Reproduced by permission of *Catalogue for Gamesmen, 1945*.)

continue so to do, in spite of repeated corrections, right up to the toss.

If his opponents possessed a star man, a celebrated player, he would elaborately never have heard of him. So far from taking any notice of trains or routes suggested by opposing club secretaries, he would demand to be met with his team at the station, at, say, 9.15, and then not arrive by train at all, but appear at the sportsground two hours later, with all his team in a charabanc.

Good work has been done lately in changing-rooms by such clubs as the Basingstoke Tusslers. The china of their washbasins is seamed and cracked. The taps are marked 'hot' and 'cold', but all that comes out of the hot tap is a long sucking noise, and unless the feet are placed at least a yard from the basin, they are resting on what seems to be mud. Instead of mirrors over the basins, there are notices saying, PLEASE LEAVE THE WASH BASINS AS YOU WOULD LIKE TO FIND THEM.

The secretary of this same Basingstoke club, the go-ahead W. Brood, later developed another device for preventing geniality in dressing-rooms. He would dress a junior groundsman in a dark suit and cause him to walk quietly through the dressing-room about twice when the Away team were in it. Later he would come up, full of apologies, to the visiting captain:

'I'm most terribly sorry – I didn't mean him to come in when you were here, but we've lost so many things from the lockers lately – nothing to do with you people, I need hardly say – that we've got this man more or less permanently on duty, watching.'

This sort of thing presented no kind of difficulty, of course, to Scott-Dickens. He knew all about Brood, and he never visited Brood or any of his Club Secretary imitators without bringing an extra 12th man whom he would introduce as 'Our detective. We've had to, you know.'

I consider Brood should have first credit for the development of Playfieldsmanship in its broader aspects. He has made a little name for Basingstoke by his keenness and dash. May I add, as a footnote to this section, that the Brood flair is very much 'in the family'. Charming Molly Brood, his daughter, is gamesmistress at Basingstoke College for Daughters of Gentlewomen. It is pretty to see how, under Molly's training, the College lacrosse team treats a visiting side. The girls stand aside in little groups, never speaking to their opponents when they arrive or when they are looking unsuccessfully for the changing-room. With their backs half-turned towards the embarrassed visitors, they will suddenly break into little screams of giggling laughter. Before Molly's advent, things were very different.

AN UNUSUAL INSTANCE

Occasionally matches are played *away by both sides*. This curious feature needs a special ploy, seen in its simplest form with Lord's Schools, who play, of course, at Lord's. The match is really fought out in the pavilion, often called the 'sacred shrine' of cricket. The side which seems to be most at ease and to know its way about best is said to have won. It is not generally known that Odoreida is an old Wykhamist.* He once managed to get into the pavilion himself for a few minutes. It was during a Lord's Schools match. Everybody heard him ask 'why the picture of Nyren had been moved from the right to the left of the glass case containing C. B. Fry's walking stick'. Later, Odoreida was seen wearing First Eleven colours. It is easy to prove he was never awarded them.

A NOTE ON GAMESMANSHIP AND THE CLASSICS

It is a great pleasure to me to be able to introduce at this early date (July 1950) a reference to the work of the Birnam Society, now centred at Wellington, Berks. In the last of my Bude lectures I spoke of Gamesmanship and Shakespeare, and though most of my remarks referred to Footnote Play I had something to say, as well, of Shakespeare himself as a gamesman. I pointed out that C. Jones had shown that the fight in the last Act of *Hamlet* was swarming with ploys (how exquisite Hamlet's 'These Foyles have all a length?' † just before the fight begins). I showed that Coriolanus was the victim of massive ploys on the part of that great gameswoman, Volumnia. I drew attention, in *Macbeth*, not only to the expensive ploy of the 'moving' of Birnam Wood to Dunsinane,

* 2 May – 6 June 1922.

† I absolutely prefer the First Folio spelling (F1).

but to the splendid Superstition Play of Macduff and the timing of his casual reference to the fact that he was

from his Mother's womb *

    Untimely Ript.

On these small beginnings the Birnam (& Dunsinane) Society was founded, with its Homership Fellowship, under the supervision of H. Wright, with whom I was up.

H. Wright (also known as 'H. H. S. Wright' or 'Root') has based his life as supervisor on the theory that Odysseus was the perfect gamesman and suggests that the epithet most often used of Odysseus – πολύμητις – should in future be translated 'gamesmanlike' instead of the feeble 'of many wiles'.

At Wellington, under 'Root's' skilful direction, results are beginning to come in. Let me reprint almost in full this note (by A. le Maitre) on the funeral games of Iliad XXIII.

The whole art of Homeric gamesmanship as typified in the chariot race is contained in the maxim : 'He, who has the best gods, wins.' It is here, surely, that we see the best and most classic examples of godmanship. It is true that the Gamesman always sticks to his rules, but rules become unnecessary if (*a*) the gods or (*b*), more important, the goddesses, are on your side. Eumelus, who had a mere male god on his side, never had a chance : Apollo may have taken Diomedes' whip and left him completely shiftless, but Athene went one better.

Not only did she give Dionysus back his whip, but she heartened his horses, and at the same time she broke Eumelus' chariot pole and ran his horses out of the race. Pallas Athene was obviously interested in the result of the race.

---

* Again, see how much more zing in F1 (the First Folio spelling).

Perhaps a little investigation of Odysseus' movements at the time would not be unprofitable!

The secondary gambit, for those not professionally acquainted with the gods and thus unable to command their interest, financial or otherwise, seems to have been plain downright dangerous driving. But we must not deprive the drivers of all credit for their gamesmanship. There is surely some significance in the fact that Antilochus rode level with Menelaus for such a distance and *only* that distance *that a discus might carry when cast for a practice throw*. Evidently there is some subtle measurement here of psychological strain. One feels that Antilochus had practised this manoeuvre time and again until he had perfected it. Students of gamesmanship will recognize in his manoeuvre a rudimentary but nevertheless definite form of the 'flurry'.

'The first muscle stiffened, is the first point gained.' With a little thought we can diagnose in Diomedes' tactics before the dramatic intervention of Athene and Phoebus Apollo a cruder application of this effective psychological gambit. We are told that Diomedes' horses were breathing 'down Eumelus' back', so close were they; here again there is an application of the flurry. To be quite accurate the word, 'μετάφρενον', means less 'back' than 'the part behind the kidneys' – a section of the body unusually susceptible to this form of irritation. It would have been interesting to see the results of this gambit. But it was not to be. Godmanship decided the issue.

THINGS YOU MAY LIKE TO KNOW

LIST OF LEADING GAMESMEN: THE LADDER

Yes, Gamesmenites, it is true that in our Yeovil office, over the Founder's desk, there is the 'Gamesman's Ladder' – the list of leading gamesmen in order of merit. There are 600 spaces but some of them are blank. Any gamesman can challenge any other gamesman *one* or *two* places above him, and if in the opinion of the Committee the lower outgames the higher, the order on the ladder is changed.

OUTPOSTS

Besides the ladder for Britain, there is a ladder for the United States of America, an international Gameswoman's Ladder, a leading Gameswoman, and a leading Gamesman for individual districts. You may be surprised to hear that there is a Paris One, a Huntercombe One, a Boston One, an Aldeburgh One. The Gamesman need never feel he is alone, and Empire bonds are strong. Wonderful links are being formed, and techniques exchanged, with all the cut and thrust of monthly correspondence. The other day, for instance, the First Gamesman for Ulster prepared a ploy in Clothesmanship which was turned down by Number One Holy Land.*

* Author of one of our first Near East publications: 'Dead Seamanship, its Practice and Exercise' (Pam: 31014).

HORSE EXERCISE
AT HOME.

WEEK-ENDMANSHIP: COUNTER GUEST PLAY. An early
device for trapping guests into 'entering into the spirit' of home
games, not being spoil-sports, and 'joining in the fun'.
See Chapter 2, page 30.   (Advertisement)

MORE ABOUT PENGUINS
AND PELICANS

Penguinews, which appears every month, contains details of all the new books issued by Penguins as they are published. From time to time it is supplemented by *Penguins in Print*, which is our complete list of almost 5,000 titles.

A specimen copy of *Penguinews* will be sent to you free on request. Please write to Dept EP, Penguin Books Ltd, Harmondsworth, Middlesex, for your copy.

In the U.S.A.: For a complete list of books available from Penguins in the United States write to Dept CS, Penguin Books, 625 Madison Avenue, New York, New York 10022.

In Canada: For a complete list of books available from Penguins in Canada write to Penguin Books Canada Ltd, 2801 John Street, Markham, Ontario L3R 1B4.